ABOUT THE AUTHOR

I am a retired Chemical Engineer with a B.S. degree from Clemson University and a Master's Degree in Financial Management from the University of North Carolina at Charlotte. The book you are about to read is an attempt to turn my technical and business writing skills into a subject that can be profitable and exciting for you.

One of my interests has been in exploring" disrupters" of business models. Amazon and Alibaba are two of the biggest disrupters, and that is what first interested me in this subject.

I hope that you will buy this book, find that it satisfies your interest in understanding the subject and that you will take the time to give this book your honest review. I will take this as encouragement for me to research other fields and write similar books.

Thank you for taking the time to read this section, and I look forward to reading your review.

BEGINNERS' GUIDE (STEP BY STEP)
TO SELLING PRIVATE LABEL PRODUCTS ON

AMAZON FBA

:: How Can I Do That?

BY

Walker L Beau-Grady

Legal Notice

Disclaimer: This book should not be interpreted as proving legal or accounting advice. Neither I nor this book is represented as qualified to do so. The comments given are for educational and information purposes only, and no claims, representations or guarantees are made of incomes resulting from the attempts to exercise suggestions made herein. Readers are expected to perform their own due diligence and contact qualified professionals for advice.

I am not affiliated with Amazon. Amazon is a trademark of Amazon.com, Inc.

Commentary on products are my own opinion and do not represent those of the creating or marketing companies or their representatives unless otherwise specified.

Software Recommendations Disclaimer:

I do make several recommendations throughout this book on software that you may find useful. They are either free (or reasonably low priced) and based on my personal experience and research. (And I do like FREE.) To be clear, no one is paying me for my recommendations. I have provided some "click throughs" in the appendices for convenience. I also provide you with enough information for you to reach the product sites with a little help from Google. I make no representations about these products and suggest that you do your own research because new and better offerings are constantly made available.

ACKNOWLEDGEMENTS

I am especially indebted to by editor, Marty. Thanks, Love.

I also want to thank Sally and Michelle, along with the other members of our "Ocala Amazon FBA Club" for their insights which made their way into this book. I wish everyone the best.

Table of Contents

PREFACE

I f you read my About the Author page, you already know that I am a retired Chemical Engineer with a B.S. degree from Clemson University and a Master's Degree in Financial Management from the University of North Carolina at Charlotte. You might be thinking that this is generally not the background of someone you would expect to write a series of books about selling on Amazon.

Similar books are often written by those who had limited experience prior to selling on Amazon, "learned by doing," made unimaginable fortunes, and continue to earn monthly what most people would consider a good living if earned annually, and all with very little effort on their part.

They just want to share their secrets with you so that you can sit on a beach in a permanent vacation mode and have Amazon bring customers to you, warehouse and ship your products, and send your profits directly into your bank accounts every two weeks. You will be able to do this in a couple of months, working only on nights and weekends, and you do not need much capital to start this amazing business. Their coaching programs will show you how. **Wow! Sign me up!**

I have no vested interest in trying to convince you that selling on Amazon will be profitable and easy. This book is not an advertisement for my other services.

This book is a product of my research, and that is all that I sell. I will show you how to make money (and many will), but I will also be clear about the new skills you need to learn and the commitment required to be a success.

This comprehensive guidebook will show you the genuine opportunities that selling on Amazon offers. You have purchased a detailed step-by-step manual on how to be successful; this includes insights into the commitment of time and resources required to achieve that success.

You will get a liberal dose of realism along the way so that you can make an informed decision about whether these risk-reward opportunities are for you. No one wants to waste their valuable time investigating opportunities that are not for them or be surprised later because the risks were not covered well enough.

You will find "off-ramps" along the way in the form of questions so that you can exit your inquiry as you learn more about the selling process. By the time you read the last chapter, you will understand all the skills and resources needed to be a success and have concluded that this opportunity is for you.

To be sure, there are profitable selling opportunities just ahead. Let's begin!

CHAPTER 1. INTRODUCTION

Y ou want to learn what selling on Amazon is all about and I hope to prepare new entrepreneurs with a **realistic overview of the opportunities and risks**. I will include all the detailed information you will need to "learn your craft" and to understand the level of commitment and resources required to succeed.

A review of the subject indicates there is substantial money to be made for those willing to learn new skill sets, and I suspect this may be the reason you have searched for my book. There are also risks involved; I have tried to point out some of them so you will not have a Pollyannaish view of the potential money to be made.

I have devoted one chapter entirely to pointing out these concerns and trying to provide guidance on how to mitigate them. After completing this book, you should have all the information you need to decide on whether this is an adventure that you wish to undertake.

To that point, I have provided "off-ramps," I call **"blue litmus paper tests,"** periodically to confirm that you want to proceed through this book knowing what we have covered so far. This opportunity is not for everyone, and I want you to know ASAP if you should continue to invest your time to learn more about this.

My emphasis on building your e-commerce business will be through selling Private Label products. That is creating your own product under your own label.

For the sustainable long term, I believe this approach offers the best opportunity for your financial success selling on Amazon.

Many of you readers may have come from an experience with selling Retail Arbitrage on Amazon, and I briefly touch on the difference between RA and selling private labels in Chapter 2. If you have that experience, it can also serve as a starting place for selling your private label products.

If any of you believe that selling other peoples' products may be of interest, please look at my book on this subject, *"**Beginners' Guide to Selling on Amazon :: Buy at Clearance Sales and Resell (Retail Arbitrage)**"*

A. Take-Aways from this Book

You will find that it takes a commitment of your time and resources, overcoming errors and bad luck, and the driving desire to succeed. Others have tried and had setbacks; this book is intended to help you avoid some of their mistakes.

The money required to succeed will not be outside the ability for most to commit; **do not risk money that you cannot afford to lose**. The time to learn new skill sets and to adopt the mindset based on the principals of all successful entrepreneurs will be the most difficult challenge.

If you develop that mindset and already have that spirit, the specific guidance in this book will help you reach your goals. I will focus on the way most of you will want to build your business.

That is not through renting warehouse space and handling large boxes of goods, hiring and supervising employees, and shipping products to distant locations. You will want to **conduct your business from your computers and phones**.

You will want someone else to perform those other labor-intensive tasks. I will concentrate on FBA, Fulfilled by Amazon, and mention other options that you may pursue to augment FBA.

Most people have found that having Amazon do the packing and shipping, handle customer complaints about damaged and delayed packages, and organize customer orders is a better and faster method to success than taking on those burdens themselves. You will learn why and how to conduct business with Amazon, and I will give you enough detail so that you will know how to do specific tasks when the time comes.

I will also recommend that you know how to access the **vast amount of information (written and video) from Amazon.** These are constantly being updated to reflect the ever-changing selling environment within Amazon.

You will learn how to access these, and you might want to view them while following along in this book. **YT (YouTube) is another excellent source** of videos on just about any specific topic associated with selling on Amazon.

One more issue that separates the building of a sustainable business from the get rich quick crowd is the idea that you will quickly be taking money out of your business to pay for those great vacations. Sorry, but this is not going to happen if you are starting with limited capital and intend to grow your business.

Growing means using your profits to buy more inventory, find new products to sell, open-up new advertising and sales or distribution methods. Every dollar that someone removes from that business reduces the ability to grow.

You may want to add money later as you see your plan succeeding, but you do not want to remove money early in the process and see your plans falter. You will know when that time has come to enjoy some of the financial rewards, but that time is not in the near term. Allow your business to tell you when this time has arrived; do not set any artificial timetables.

B. Litmus Test for Success

You are not reading this book purely for enjoyment or the love of a good story. You want to know if selling on Amazon is something you would be interested in pursuing, and you should want to know that as soon as possible.

I am going to tell you what you will need to do to be successful. From that, you should be able to determine if you will commit to be a success.

Do not be concerned about not having all the technical skills required for each task involved; most of these can be outsourced online and for only a few dollars. Learning to outsource needed services will be one of the skill sets you will learn.

If this clearly is not for you, I want to provide "off ramps" well before you reach the last chapter. So how do you know right now if this is likely something that will excite you? Is there an off-ramp for you now?

If only there were a simple little test, a **litmus paper test** that would turn blue for those destined for success. Well I happen to have one and here is Your Litmus Test:

- You need to "understand the basics of business" before learning to sell on Amazon. Most of you reading this book have this, whether it is by practice, reading, education, or working for a business.

- Willingly keep a spreadsheet up to date with all the data you will need to collect and analyze. You will find the specifics of your spreadsheet as you learn various skill sets, but you must keep records.

- Keep current on what you believe your level of commitment needs to be as you read each chapter. (Taking notes would be nice.) Be willing to devote the time and resources for success.

- **Install a Chrome browser add-on called "Keepa,"** and judge this to be an "exciting" window into selling on Amazon. Yes, please do this now; this will be your little gift for reading to this point, and a reminder of your selling potential every time to shop on Amazon.

Open your Chrome browser and search for "chrome extensions." Search for **"Keepa amazon price,"** and install.

Every time you go to an Amazon product page, you will see a graph of historical selling prices and the number of sellers with this product for sale.

If you find this knowledge "exciting," the kind of activity you want to engage with, then this could be for you. If you do not see the point, then I suggest that **your litmus paper is not blue**. And you are welcome!

C. The First Six Months

It was July, and 35 class members spent $995 each to attend a three-day seminar by experts who would show us how they and their students succeeded in creating an **additional $10,000 a month of income**. It turns out that this could be done "right here in River City," in a few months for a few work hours a week, with little capital, from home, and with practically no risk.

These guys were very good at selling the American dream! They were also good at selling "coaching packages" to help you reach your dream.

A few class members paid really-big bucks for additional coaching. Others of us decided that we could do this ourselves and formed a support group that met weekly to get everyone up to speed so we could ultimately go our own way.

The group felt good that a couple of those who paid for additional coaching also joined the group. We shared the benefits of this coaching, but my personal takeaway was of the very limited benefits derived from that expensive "personal" coaching.

The original group-thinking was that we first learn the Amazon system by selling Retail Arbitrage (most found RA very easy to do) and then move to Private Labels. By Christmas, some members had sold several thousand dollars each on Amazon and felt confident that we had learned the system without additional coaching.

Based on this experience, I am convinced that a good book on the subject will give you the resources to learn the details, understand the concepts and the commitments involved. Having all the needed information available to you in one place so that you can reference the details as needed, is far better than taking notes from a phone conversation.

So why, of the 17 originally in this support group, did only a few remain after the Christmas selling season to pursue private labels? It was not because of what they learned about the opportunities, but what they learned about themselves and their level of commitments.

As each one left, the reason was not that they no longer believed that making money was possible. I did not hear that from anyone.

Most had made some money with RA and understood that the major profits would be from selling private labels. Studying the group for clues, my conclusion was that most, if not all, of those leaving after Christmas would not have found their litmus paper to be blue.

Many did not have a background in business and had never used a spreadsheet. Others were smart and capable and experienced in business, but most of those leaving felt that the time demands were more than they were willing or able to commit along with their current jobs. Yes, and there were **those who did not see the point of that Keepa graph**.

I give you this story because you should take those elements of the litmus test seriously and apply them to your situation. Make note of your analysis at the end of each chapter and compare this to your commitment to this effort.

Did you notice that I did not tell you how much money you can make by selling on Amazon? I have no clue. The money to be made will **depend entirely on your level of commitment.**

D. How to Use this Book

I have "packed" this book with the details of what you will need to become successful selling on Amazon. Because of the detail presented, I strongly suggest that you read this book for the first time to **get an overview of the subject**. Do not be overly concerned with the detail during your fist reading, but concentrate on the nature of the work and effort required of you.

I expect that you will use this as a reference book where you can refer to specific chapters for review and find other sources to enhance your knowledge beyond what I covered in those chapters. For the most part, each chapter follows the previous in a chronological series breaking down the subjects into manageable subsets.

There are Appendices where you will find more tables containing data on specific costs, software suggestions, and using Amazon University. The Table of Contents will give you a breakdown of the general topics to make it easier to search later.

Beyond that, topics are covered so that you can gain a sense of the overall profit potential, risk capital needed, dangers that may not be obvious, and the commitments needed to be successful. I encourage you to "**read ahead**" by skimming upcoming chapters to put what you have read in context.

I probably should be encouraging all my readers to complete the book before rendering a decision on whether selling on Amazon is right for you. The truth is that you probably should complete the book before deciding, but that some of you will know early on that this is not for you.

I respect that and suggest that after each chapter, you take the time to assimilate this new information and create your own litmus tests. The basics are not that difficult, and you are capable of succeeding.

Since you passed the first "blue litmus paper" test above, I hope that you will remain until you have read the last chapter on an In-Depth Analysis of Competitors. That is a very technical approach to an important subject, but I made this the last chapter to be read only by those most likely to succeed.

E. Software Recommendations

I do make several recommendations throughout this book on software that you will find useful, like Keepa. They are **either free or reasonably low priced** and based on my personal experience and research. (And I do like FREE.)

To be clear, no one is paying me for my recommendations. Accordingly, I generally avoided providing "click-throughs" directly to these product sites (except in the appendices for convenience) because that is how authors often receive compensation for products.

I do not believe the use of these affiliate links is a bad practice, and I may do this in other books, but I wanted there to be no doubt about the reason I made these recommendations. I make no representations about these products and suggest that you do your own research because new and better offerings are constantly made available.

I do provide you with enough information for you to reach the product sites with a little help from Google. You can find a **complete list of this software in Appendix A**.

CHAPTER 2. THE OLD AND THE NEW SUPPLY CHAINS

Today the wholesalers and distributors are feeling the impact of retailers going directly to manufacturers to source their goods. The traditional supply chain is becoming less viable, more at risk from the online disrupters, and this is blurring the lines between retailers and the rest of the supply chain.

Why is this happening? The prices and delivery dates to the online retailer are lower than using the traditional supply chain. Two of the principle disrupters driving this change are **Alibaba and Amazon**.

A.   The Disruptors

Online retailers are also avoiding the high costs of brick and mortar stores to deliver goods at a very competitive price to consumers while making more profit. The winners are the customers and those retailers flexible enough to adjust to the realities of the new, and evolving supply chain.

1.   Alibaba and Amazon

Sites like **Alibaba** make inexpensive manufacturers' products directly available to millions of retailers so they can buy products at lower volumes for prices only slightly higher than those sold to distributors. These prices are generally less than those available from traditional wholesalers. There are **MOQ (Minimum Order Quantity)** requirements, but these MOQs are now affordable for most retailers.

A combination of the lower cost of goods, shorter lead times and reduced overhead make the online retailer competitive with even the largest of local retailers.

And the exciting part is that these manufacturers will make products to your specifications, creating your own private labeled product.

The other disruptor is **Amazon**, a site where small retailers, called third-party sellers", have access to millions of potential customers. While Amazon sources and sells some of the products you find there, most of the sellers are third parties, many small sellers. You probably pay little attention to the seller's name when ordering, but look carefully next time, and you will often find the names of many retailers, large and small, selling the same or similar products.

Most of these small retailers are selling to **Prime customers with two-day delivery**. That would be nearly impossible for them without the clout of behemoth Amazon supporting their sales.

This (constantly evolving) retail business model has also attracted individuals into a retail arena where they had no previous experience. The primary attraction is the ability for individuals to compete effectively with the established brick and mortar retailer without the outlay of large sums of money.

These new players only need to learn the skill sets required by this evolving business model and be willing to commit their time and resources to be successful. This little book will explain the concepts involved, introduce you to the skill sets required, and provide the necessary instructions to make them part of your personal toolbox.

The work required to turn these into your personal success story is your commitment to reaching your goals. Seriously, the concepts are easily understandable, and the practice is not difficult, but this is a journey into starting a business online which requires **discipline and commitment**. "And that ain't nothing."

2. Why Sell on Amazon

Amazon is e-commerce! Small independent business operators, whether retail or business-to-business, need to be involved. Whether you decide to partner with Amazon or not, your competitors will be doing so in increasing numbers.

They will use their existing supply chain in the beginning, then develop new ones with Alibaba while accessing millions of Amazon customers. They will learn the skill sets involved, and they will learn how to exploit the unique sales tools that Amazon provides to their most successful sellers.

To be clear, the large profits by Amazon are driven, in part, by independent sellers who list on their site. Amazon takes their cut of your sales, so there is every incentive for them to use their considerable resources to help you succeed.

The **Amazon Sellers Central and Sellers University** with their videos, chat, email and phone support are excellent resources. Their **Sellers Forum** is another source where you learn from other sellers. Learning their requirements, how to submit inventory, and how to use their reports are typical of the basic skill sets that require you to spend the time to explore the Amazon sites.

B. Two Common Selling Strategies

There are many derivations of the common selling strategies on Amazon, and this is not meant to describe all of them, but the concepts behind Retail Arbitrage and Private Labels are the principal ones. It is useful to understand the major differences in selling strategies for beginning sellers on Amazon.

1. Retail Arbitrage

Despite the strange sounding name, retail arbitrage is the easiest way to get started on Amazon. Arbitrage simply means that you take advantage of price differences in different markets, different stores.

You buy low from the store having a clearance sale and sell higher in your Amazon store. That's it; that is retail arbitrage, and it is just that simple. I started there, and most sellers begin there.

You do not need a lot of money, and most people can find the time to perform some level of this. I will not spend any time on the details of this strategy beyond telling you that I have written a book on the subject and invite you to buy a copy on Amazon. See **"Beginners' Guide (Step By Step) to Selling on Amazon (Retail Arbitrage): Buy at Clearance Sales and Resell on Amazon FBA (Fulfilled By Amazon)"**.

2. Private Labels

Imagine selling **your own products!** Have you considered a product that showcases your creativity, with your design, your logo (perhaps, "from the house of Michelle")? Well, don't get too carried away because there are limitations if you plan on selling a successful product on Amazon (more to follow).

You can modify and improve the right product with your touch and sell it as your own because it will be unique to you. You can find your manufacturer in China who will take care of the shipping details directly to an Amazon warehouse. That subject will be discussed in detail later.

The **proven way to be successful on Amazon** over the long term is by selling your private label products. Source your product with your logo (your design) directly on your product and your packaging.

No one else will be allowed to sell your product, so your competition will be reduced. You will not need to compete by lowering your price a few pennies to move your product to compete on price with others selling the same product.

For my readers with a background in RA, the major drawbacks (compared to RA) are that:

- Private labels will have higher start-up costs.

- Require that you launch a campaign to sell your new product.

- You must learn additional skill sets.

But the returns are worth that extra effort when done correctly. Caution: you will likely lose money if you do this without the proper understanding, planning, and execution. This book is designed to help you avoid such pitfalls.

You will have resources to learn the details, understand the concepts and the commitments involved. Ultimately, you can develop the confidence to be successful, but all the success (and all the losses) will be yours and yours alone.

Consider this statement and its sentiments and bring realistic expectations, not hope-filled naivete, to this venture. Note: I will not even return the price of this book if you fail.

How does selling private labels work?

- You design your private label product to be better than the competitions' in consultation with your Chinese manufacturer. You will learn how to do this in Chapters 5 through 7.

- You will list your Private Label product on the Amazon website and later promote it on Amazon. You will learn the details of this in Chapters 8 and 9.

- When you are ready to send your inventory, sign into your sellers central account; Amazon will provide you with the shipping documents needed to send any inventory you may have to their warehouses.

- You may elect to have your Private Label product shipped directly to Amazon warehouses in the U.S. The manufacturer can handle the shipment and all the import paperwork while you pay any import fees.

- Amazon shoppers place an order for your product and Amazon packs and ships the order. Amazon will process the money, and after subtracting their fees, money will be deposited into your checking account every two weeks.

- Repeat the process with fewer mistakes and improved efficiency. Build your business one product at a time.

C. Creating Your Amazon Seller Account

There **are two types of "Sellers Accounts" on Amazon**. The first is free, and where I recommend that you begin as an individual.

As a small individual seller, you will not be charged any ongoing costs, just a fee of $0.99 for each sales transaction. You will be able to browse around the services available and practice some of the skill sets we will discuss concerning listing products, contacting Amazon support to discuss issues that may not be clear, and integrating free software useful to sellers with your first product.

1. Opening an Individual Sellers Account

Opening a sellers account will allow you to access the resources available to you from Amazon, and there are many. At this point, you are not committing any funds, but this is an important part of understanding whether you want to go forward with a commitment.

If you have an existing Amazon account as a customer or prime member, go to "Accounts and Lists"> Your Accounts and follow the "Sellers" tabs to sign up. You can also contact Amazon to assist you with this process, and I recommend that you do so as part of learning how to work with the Amazon representatives.

I screwed up my first attempt so badly by trying to create an account with my LLC that it could not be altered (because it had not been completed properly), and it could not be deleted. That attempt is still hanging out there in limbo today.

After reading this book for the first time to get an overview of everything involved, consider signing up for an individual account as your first step. An individual account will minimize your costs and allow you to become familiar with Sellers Central and the mechanics of selling on Amazon.

If you decide to create an LLC or other company later, you can change your account to your company name when you get to that stage. Most of the sign-up information can be changed later.

An exception to that is your email address. **Create a new email address** specifically for your communications with Amazon about your business.

2. Opening a Professional Account

You can upgrade your free individual account to a professional account for $39.99 per month when you are ready. You would be charged $0.99 per item sold with your individual account, but you can sell without this per item charge with the professional account.

You will want to upgrade to a professional account before you are ready to send your first private label order to Amazon. You can create your own product listings, access reports, and interface your account with third-party software.

In either account, you can begin selling on the Amazon e-commerce platform to Prime customers from Amazon warehouses. This is where your products will be FBA (Fulfilled By Amazon). I cannot overstate the huge advantages of being able to sell to the Prime customers and taking advantage of Amazon's low shipping costs:

- Two years ago, 60% of buyers searched exclusively for Prime products (free shipping and two-day delivery). That percentage is likely larger today and growing.

- Your cost of shipping to an Amazon warehouse will be 50-80% below the private cost to ship.

CHAPTER 3. UNDERSTANDING PRIVATE LABELING

The advantages of having your own product will make this a better long-term investment of your time than RA, or any other approach to online selling. There is **simply more profit is selling your own product** than someone else's.

You will be in control of your product and a leader in your market niche. For most of you, this will be a new, and potentially incredible business model that can create profits, consistent with your ability to harness the skill sets involved.

- You will select your own product, one that has improvements over the competition. I will show you how to do this.

- Place your own logo on the product along with packaging that makes your product unique.

- You will select a product with high profit margins and not have to reduce your price by a few pennies to compete in your niche.

- You will select a niche with similar products that are selling well, and you should expect to be very competitive with them over a few weeks.

- The high profit margin and high sales will give you room to become even more competitive.

- You can build a product line with related products for sale on Amazon, other platforms, and your own website.

A. Why Source from China Using Alibaba?

Many of us would like to source of our products here are in our own country. (We are all patriots, right?) However, as a business owner, you must source product where you get the quality necessary to compete at a reasonable (low) cost.

Each country has different resources, infrastructure, government policies, and real estate features that affect their economic competitiveness. Sourcing from China has advantages for Amazon sellers because of a large number of factories making products for export all over the world, and **their government subsidizes those exports**.

Another way to look at this is that what you will pay for most consumer goods is artificially low because part of the cost has been paid by the Chinese worker. (Note that China is not currently subsidizing precision machine tools nor wheat exports, but other countries are, and you will know this by their low prices.)

Yes, transportation costs are always a factor to consider. Even with this added cost of transporting goods from overseas, you will almost always find that the cost of imported manufactured goods will be less than those produced domestically.

To keep prices low and bypass purchasing from a distributor, there will be a **MOQ (Minimum Order Quantity)** which must be purchased. You can reduce your costs from the same supplier by purchasing larger quantities, and you should expect to do that as your sales grow.

Another big advantage is that you can access multiple factories at one time through the Alibaba platform online. This is a marketplace where you shop for suppliers, finding the ones willing to provide you with the quality and the price for your business to be successful.

Just post an **RFQ (Request For Quote),** and within 24 hours, you will have responses from English speaking representatives of those manufacturers interested in discussing your needs. You will see just how easy this is in Chapter 7; I have provided a template letter for your first contact.

B. How Much Money do I Need?

I am going to cover this in excruciating detail later in the appropriate chapters on Private Labeling products. I am lightly mentioning this issue now so that you will have some idea as to whether this is a viable concept for you.

I am not concerned that you would not be successful because of limited experience selling. If you complete this book, you should understand what will be required and be able to compare that to your abilities.

You will discover how to calculate the amount of money you will need depending on the MOQ (Minimum Order Quantity), the cost delivered to an Amazon warehouse, and the delivery time from your supplier compared to the turnover rate. You will also require money to promote your new product.

Those are all controllable factors, but it is not in the hundreds; it is in the thousands. A small operation might be $5,000, but **a minimum of $10,000** would be much more comfortable for most start-ups.

C. Existing Brick and Mortar Store Owners

I want to address the issue about the long-term viability of small businesses selling exclusively from a storefront operation. I am not from this background but discussing this issue with some who are and reading the literature on this issue; many suggest that some online presence will be required to remain viable.

You may have already opened your own website, or you may have tried Shopify or eBay. In that case, you would be known as a "click and mortar" store.

Amazon may not be the best platform for you, but this juggernaut is on its way to becoming the dominant seller in many markets. No new malls have been built in the U.S., and existing properties are being "re-imagined," or closed.

Did Amazon play a large role in that? If Amazon sales have done this to the big-money retail players, how is your small business going to adapt?

Consider what happened last year when Amazon began competing with grocery items, prescription drugs, and other drugstore items. I remember when Amazon was just an online bookseller.

Just saying, you should find out if this platform will work for you. **Being a part of this commerce gobbling behemoth** may be better than competing against it.

D. Business Setup

Existing business owners most often just make this a part of that business. You may have existing employees who can be re-tasked to handle much of the packing, labeling, and inventory. If you do not have talented internet people, those skills can be hired on a part-time basis, or online (discussed later with virtual assistants) on a low-cost ad hoc basis.

You also have the advantage of possibly selling existing inventory at profitable prices. One of my pharmacy friends sells a couple of over the counter items at higher margins through Amazon than through the pharmacy.

Once you understand the selling expenses at Amazon, check out some of your inventory to see if any would be profitable. You may be surprised at what some people will pay for the convenience of buying a product with 2-day delivery directly to their home.

For those without an existing business entity, there are several options. Many individuals use **an LLC for ease of paperwork and the costs** involved.

In Florida, you can apply online and have the paperwork within a week for $150 plus annual costs. The cost in California is over $800 annually.

Using an LLC will isolate your personal assets from your business dealings. An LLC also allows you **to open a bank account** in the name of your business and **set up credit cards** accordingly.

I also suggest that you **open a PayPal account** associated with the bank account at the same time. You will likely need that later in the process when dealing with potential suppliers about samples.

E.   An Overview of the Heart of This Book

Why read the details needed for success when you can just read a summary, think "Cliffs Notes"? (Raise your hand if you made it through high school literature that way.) I want to give you an overview early in the process so you can keep in mind the process and skills needed to be successful.

Chapter 4 details how to **define the type of product you want to create** as a Private Label. You will find out about your personal product niche and the financial considerations of your choice.

Chapter 5 will show you the use of software to search the hundreds of millions of potential products selling on Amazon **to find the one that is your best potential PL product**. Doing this without the aid of software would be an impossible task for the beginner.

In Chapter 6 you will take that generic PL product and **create your personal PL with a product name, logo and package**. You will find out about branding, trademarks, and adding additional value to your product.

Chapter 7 will show you how to **find a reliable supplier in China** and negotiate the manufacturing of your private label product to your specifications. You will learn about the first contact with your supplier (including a first-contact template letter) all the way through the delivery to Amazon warehouses.

Chapter 8 will show you **how to create a great listing page** on Amazon so that customers can find your Private Label. This listing page will be the key to converting Amazon customers into your customers.

Chapter 9 will provide detailed instructions on **how to launch your product** to compete effectively with other sellers quickly. You will learn the advertising skills needed for the initial launch and the ongoing advertising effort both within and outside the Amazon platform.

Chapter 10 expands upon the risk-reward issues of selling your PL product to include a separate discussion devoted exclusively to **concerns about dealing with Amazon**. You will find both concerns and ways to minimize those concerns.

Chapter 11 deals with **expanding your Amazon success** into global sales, and selling in other venues. You will find other online sales platforms to build on your Amazon sales, and perhaps increase your ROI on those sales.

Chapter 12 highlights additional methods for **driving outside traffic to your site** and your product. You can significantly improve sales and profits using the Amazon Affiliate Program, Google searches, and YT videos.

Chapter 13 is about **analyzing your competition**. This chapter may seem out of order, and it is, but it is so technical that I wanted you to understand the overall process first.

I wanted you to commit selling, knowing this is for you before you spent the time to understand this amount of detail. I assume that if you read this chapter, then you are very interested and that I did not discourage you by introducing realist issues into this discussion during the first 12 chapters.

F.   Short Cuts to Creating Your Private Label

You can see from the above list of skills that this process will take some time and effort. Surely, there must be some way to create a private label and sell it on Amazon without committing to so much work.

Yes, there is! Kole Imports and others will make it easy for you and you will not need to take possession of the product directly at any time. They will handle all the physical issues related to your product.

Find one of their current imports that you can buy at a price that ensures you can sell at a profit. Review their online catalog and compare to similar items now being sold on Amazon.

Use the estimate of one-third for your cost compared to the selling price as a starting point to avoid the tedious calculations involved to see what the actual expenses and profits are. Contact Kole to see if they will allow you to sell this product as your own private label.

Buy a small quantity and have Kole place your private label on the product (perhaps your logo "sticker") and send it directly to an Amazon warehouse. Kole can add all labels and wrap the product as required so that it is ready for sale when it reaches an Amazon warehouse.

You can create your listing and see how it compares to the listings of others. You could change the price and make other changes to see how sales respond. You will be able to see how it sells and whether there is an ongoing profit to be made.

If you find a product that works for you, Kole might order it with your logo and even add product changes to improve it. They will handle all the importing issues.

I discussed this with Amazon, and they had no problem with the concept, but you should do the same once you have a specific product in mind. You may have found an easy way to create your private label product, and Kole will deal with the suppliers for you.

You can find suppliers that will sell you creams and lotions, vitamin supplements, hair products, and so much more. What could possibly go wrong with that business model?

At this point you have created a private label product with:

- No existing demand for your label.

- Unknown quality (definitely not the higher quality that you need to be successful).

- You introduced an additional cost layer between you and the manufacturer.

- You still have to put in all the costs and effort to create a demand.

- Finally, you will have a cost structure higher than the competition because you are placing another profit-making company between you and your source.

Such an approach is not a recipe for success. To be clear, I am not seriously suggesting that you seek out shortcuts as a viable business model.

This exercise was proposed as a concept to allow you to better analyze some of the offers you may find. Any concept that adds another layer between you and your supplier or your customer needs to be viewed with suspicion.

Creating your own Private label, with your own design and improvements, is what I am advocating, and not just to have any product with your name on it. **It is time to begin.**

CHAPTER 4. WHAT DOES YOUR PRIVATE LABEL PRODUCT LOOK LIKE

I f you open a book on private labels that begin with "type brackets, "[ ]" into the search bar at Amazon, this book is dated, but it still may have useful information and concepts. The idea was that Amazon would show you the top-selling products by category using this technique.

While selling well for one characteristic you want in a product, that is only one of many search criteria you need when searching a database with several hundred million products. This approach may not be the best use of your valuable time compared to using software that only returns products meeting several search criteria.

While well-meaning, that specific technique has not worked for years. However, a similar technique is available to show the best-selling products in a category. Type "best selling baby toys for boys age 4" in the search bar. You might find this useful after you have mastered the structured approaches in this chapter, and you understand the many characteristics you want in a product.

You will always be **looking for potential new products** once you are a private label seller on Amazon. This is not the technique for beginners, but you will know when you might find this useful as an experienced seller.

When selling retail arbitrage and wholesale products, third-party sellers were primarily using other sellers' listings, selling the same products they had been selling. You could use their work to some extent, and enjoy the customers who were already looking for that product. With your own private label, you need to do all of that from the beginning, plus more.

So why would you want to do that? You want that **because you will have much less competition**. You can establish your price without contending with the same product being sold for a few cents less. If you do it right, you will have a superior product and create a listing that will draw customers to your detail page.

Once on your page, you should expect to close the sale because you have provided a solution to the reason they came to your page initially. And they have no reason to search for a similar product (More about that in Chapter 9 on Listing Your Product).

There is a structured approach to the process of finding products for sale that will maximize your profit potential and minimize your time to search through potential products. Fortunately, there is also software to aid in this process.

A.   The Products You Want to Sell

You have complete control over selecting your product at this stage. Do not squander this opportunity! Once you have selected it, your control begins to diminish as external factors like your suppliers, the marketplace, and your competitors exert more influence over sales. Use the control you have now to insist that you have the best possible start to succeed.

1.   High and Durable Demand

You want products with high demand. Amazon is a great marketplace for selling products which already have a demand; this is not a great market for introducing new products where you must invest heavily to increase demand.

None of us has a crystal ball to divine the future, but ask yourself if the existing demand will likely remain high for several years. You are going to invest your time and money into a product that should remain a source of income for years, so you are not looking for a fad that you expect will fade away in a year or two. For those reasons, you also do not want a product that is strictly a seasonal item; you want substantial sales every month.

You will also want to review the trends over time to select a product that is increasing in demand. Google Trends (included in software described later) will help you do that. You want the mega sales factors like demographics and consumer buying trends to be in your favor and to drive underlying sales growth into the foreseeable future.

1. No User Manual

Select a product that is obvious as to how it is used and does not require a complicated user manual. You do not want to educate the consumer on how to use what you are selling.

Whether a consumer is currently using that product or not, they should instantly know how they would use it to improve their lives or the lives of others simply by seeing a picture of it. And yes, the pictures on your Amazon listing will be one of your primary selling tools for that reason.

2. Easily Described

Your product should have **a keyword or phrase that EVERYONE would use to describe this product.** For example, everyone would use the term "baby blanket" to describe a baby blanket.

Run this test in your mind to see that consumers could find your product with an easily imagined keyword. If you mentally start your product keyword description by saying "the thing that is used for....", drop this idea and move on.

B. Understanding A Product Niche

You will first create a list of potential products that meet some basic criteria (using software) while filtering out those that might look great at first glance but have characteristics that would make it unnecessarily difficult to overcome. Instead, you need to find your product in a product niche that will eventually become "your personal product niche."

Your niche is the market you are going to break into quickly by moving into the top 9 with a superior product. You want to appear on the first page (top 9) when customers make searches. You will also want an outstanding Listing, and appropriate advertising campaign to do this. From here you will launch your drive to get the Buy Box on your product page.

The Buy Box is the listing shown first when a buyer searches for a product. You are much more likely to sell your product when you appear there. We will discuss the factors that will eventually place you there, and we begin by **defining your product niche**.

1. Product Reviews

You want to sell products in a market that is established but does not have many sellers with over 200-500 reviews. The **more reviews the better established the seller;** they are likely doing more things well, making it harder for you to compete.

You will also find that higher sales and more reviews often go together. Finding your product niche will require many hours of work on the front end of this process, but it is one of the most important decisions you will make in this process. That market is there, and it just takes persistence to find it.

2. Monthly Sales

You want sales in your niche to be high enough for you to be profitable without staring out selling more than anyone else. You also want a reasonable number of competitors selling in that same category.

The way I try to nail this down is by using numbers to describe this niche. My point is not that you memorize these numbers; they are just guidelines to help you as you are starting out. Concentrate instead on the concepts involved.

Your product **niche should have total sales of more than 1800-3600 per month** for the largest 9 sellers; that is equivalent to sales averaging more than 200 units per seller. You can compete with as many as 18 active sellers in this range of sales, but your effort goes up quickly as the number exceeds 9, the number shown on the first screen of a product search. If you find fewer competitors, this is even better.

If there are 12 competitors with one or two dominant players, average the monthly sales for the next 8 or 7 sellers to find your niche. You have dismissed the top players, for now, and know your initial sales goal. Meeting that goal should place you on the first page of search results where over 60% of sales are made.

If you are lucky enough or diligent enough to find a niche with no dominant players, and fewer than nine competitors, the math becomes easier and so do the challenges. However, there should be enough successful competitors to prove the market is viable and growing, and will provide you with the flexibility to experiment within that niche. I would want to know a great deal about a market that only had a couple of successful competitors and few reviews before committing to it, but I would chase that one down.

3. Extended Search Strategy

Before I leave this topic, I want to add that you might find a product, like a bicycle seat, that does not fit your model because there are just too many well-established sellers with many hundreds of reviews. However, if you expanded your search to a smaller segment of that market, like those made with a given material, you might find a niche within that larger market that does meet your criteria. Many potentially profitable products can be found as subsets within high volume markets using similar search techniques.

Identifying your product within this niche is what the processes in this chapter are intended to do. Understand the processes so that you will know the results will be reliable, and you will be able to "pull the trigger" to commit your capital and your time. I would suggest that you do not commit your money to a product unless you have confidence in your process and your work.

To build your confidence, use an iterative process of searches, improving your data collection each time, looking for a product better than your last one. After several searches, learning more each time, you will know that you have found the product that will be your first success.

C. Financial Considerations

Small businesses **fail far more often from inadequate financial planning** than any other reason. It is too easy to become excited about potential opportunities and rush ahead only to find that cash flow problems crushed all their other hard work.

To help you in this area, I will often mention the data that need to go into a spreadsheet so you can keep up with the most important inventory cash flow factors. The business start-up and overhead costs I leave to your experience to include.

1. Funds for Inventory

You certainly want enough sales to meet your objectives, and you want a margin that provides a reasonable profit for your efforts. However, remember that you need to fund the inventory, and a hypothetical product that cost you $10 delivered to an Amazon warehouse selling 10 units a day will cost you $3,000 for one month's inventory.

You should initially target for **enough inventory to avoid running out** before your next shipment arrives. Losing your sales position may be expensive to recover, and you will have missed profits.

For many products shipped by ocean freight from China, where delivery takes weeks, you could be placing your next inventory order before you have received much of your first month's sales revenue from Amazon. This hypothetical product idea looks like it might require $6,000 to fund the first two month's inventory.

If you can source a product that is very light and small, as recommended for your initial searches, you might be able to air freight your first MOQ. This could reduce your shipping time by weeks.

Shipping by air freight also can reduce the funds you need to purchase inventory if you work out the reorder details with your supplier to accommodate a faster delivery schedule. Look at the numbers to see what makes sense for your product, sales, and order delivery times.

I strongly recommend a spreadsheet to do this. Put hypotheticals into this spreadsheet so that you know what funds are required as the sales situation evolves. Flying by the seat of your pants on inventory control is a strategy for crash and burn.

2.   ROI (Return on Investment)

You should want approximately **80% to 120% return on your cost of goods** delivered to Amazon but would settle for less depending on the other profitability factors. For example, turning over your inventory quickly is very important. Selling twice the number of units with 75% return at the same price is 50% more profit than the 100% return.

You want a good return, but do not get too fixated on a specific number; there are other equally significant factors involved, as you will see. However, your initial criteria for an acceptable ROI (Return on Investment) should be relatively high to account for unforeseen costs and unexpected competition, so that you can protect your investment.

Calculate the ROI by dividing the profit by your "landed cost." What you must pay to have the goods arrive and go into inventory at Amazon is your "landed cost."

I have assumed that you understand business basics, so you know they include the manufacture, shipping into the country, government fees, transport from the port to an Amazon warehouse, and any preparation fees by Amazon. Not to worry, all costs will be discussed, and your supplier will handle most of these on your behalf.

I have found that these post-manufacturing cost may add as much as 20% to most products. These costs will vary widely depending on your product, but I suggest 20% only as an order of magnitude number when you are creating a spreadsheet without product-specific information. Use a spreadsheet very early in the process to collect data during the product search phase even though specific values are not available at this stage.

3. Create a Spreadsheet

While each product and niche will have inventory dynamics that vary substantially, use the above estimates while you consider your niche. And "do the math" for your product supply chain to know how much money will be required for inventory and advertising your product.

Collect the information for this calculation as you go through the process of finding your product. You want to update your capital needs and know what impact your decisions are placing on your finances.

I am an avid fan of **estimating throughout this process** so that there are no surprises near the end of this product selection process. Use generous cost estimates and constantly revise as you find other expenses, then replace them with more reliable values as your knowledge grows. It is better to over-estimate costs and miss an opportunity than under-estimate and lose your time and money.

It should be obvious from our hypothetical product example that the more product you sell initially, and the larger the per unit acquisition costs, the larger your capital requirements will be to get started. As you begin to bank profits from Amazon sales (deposited every two weeks directly into your bank account of record with Amazon), you might think that you could use these funds to reduce your capital requirements for inventory.

This is true up to a point. Consider what happens if you also begin to sell more each month; and certainly, that is the game plan. Therefore, this process of controlling inventory and providing capital to account for future sales and advertising will be ongoing.

4. Know Your Numbers

Following up on the constant need **to know your finances, "know your numbers."** Do not be one of the statistics of small companies that failed because of inadequate financial planning despite having adequate sales revenue.

Create a spreadsheet at the end of this chapter to see what your estimated sales and costs are projected to be each month for the first six-months of operation. You will be adding lines and revising costs as you go through the processes in each chapter.

The spreadsheet should be your controlling document, so keep it updated, and you will make better decisions throughout the process. Know what impact your product selection, expected sales, sourcing, supply chain dynamics, advertising, and product launching will have on your capital requirements.

Creating this spreadsheet is your feedback that you understand and are quantifying the important factors you need to be successful. If you find that the money required is more than you have, you will need to borrow money, or partner with another person, or reduce your inventory.

Reducing your inventory has such potentially negative consequences should you completely run out that I would not consider it. In addition to inventory, you also have the cost of a new product launch (although on a limited scale) and ongoing advertising costs which will become items in your spreadsheet of costs.

CHAPTER 5. YOUR BEST POTENTIAL PL PRODUCT

You are not going to create an original product that is unlike any other. You are going to find products that sell well on Amazon, but need to be improved to sell even better. So how do you find these products from among the millions of products being sold?

A. Create a list of potential product Ideas

If you have been waiting for **the fun part**, here it is. You need to sort through the Amazon database and create a general list of these products.

From that list, you need to evaluate them individually to find the best ones meeting your criteria. I will discuss some of these criteria later in this chapter, but this process becomes very individualized base on your goals, comfort level for risk-taking, and capital available.

1. Product Search Software

Fortunately, there is software available to help you do some of the heavy lifting by suggesting products that meet some of these quantitative qualities. The two free or low-cost programs that I find personally very helpful are Amazeowl and Jungle Scout.

Both have many hours of tutorials showing how to use their software on YT (YouTube). I am fans of both Seth Kniep (YouTube videos on Amazeowl) and Greg Mercer (Jungle Scout creator) and their detailed, enthusiastic teaching styles.

I find searching for potential products one of the more enjoyable activities of private labeling. Once I spent the time needed with YT to understand the software, and conducted a few searches, I wanted to spend more time than I had available searching for products.

The goal was to find an ever more promising product. But at some point, you need to stop and commit.

I want to interject **another "blue litmus" test** at this point. (I know that I said that I would let you do this after each chapter.) If you are the type of individual who wants to create a new product, completely different from others you have seen, you may not find this process of searching for existing products satisfying.

However, the process of searching for successful products, improving them and bringing them to market is what being a third-party seller on Amazon is all about. If this does not excite you, your litmus paper may not be blue.

The following are the two software systems to consider. Both are low cost and provide similar mechanical methods for finding potential products.

- Amazeowl is free software that allows you to select criteria appropriate for your business model to search the Amazon database and find products that meet your needs. You can pay for an annual add-on that makes this software even easier to use by subscribing to their "database" which I recommend you do at some point.

- JS (Jungle Scout) has a very good paid software package including their chrome extension (for a one-time fee) and web-based software for a modest monthly fee. By investing in both, you will have a product search system that is very easy to use and save you a lot of time.

Both systems are excellent at finding potential products. Each has its strengths compared to the other, and that will ultimately be a matter of personal preference. Your initial searches using JS can include factors not available with Amazeowl, and locating all results of your initial search will be easier than the free version of Amazeowl.

Using the paid "database" of Amazeowl makes it very user-friendly for finding products meeting your search criteria. Comparing Amazeowl and JS, you will also find more data for detailed analysis directly with the Amazeowl platform.

For example, you can see what similar products (and costs) are available from Alibaba without submitting a formal quote. You will also be able to better analyze the competition in your product niche directly from the Amazeowl platform (see chapter 13).

2. Amazeowl Initial Search Criteria

Amazeowl search criteria are shown below. I suggest that you initially identify products based on the criteria below and then begin to experiment to see the impact on your search results. I present these suggestions only as a starting point, and with the expectations that you will experiment later to see the impacts on your search results.

1. Optimal price range ($15 to $60)

2. The optimal range of reviews (0 to 500)

3. Maximum product weight (less than one pound)

4. Maximum product size (dimensions of less than 18 x 14 x 8 inches)

5. High sales (use the AmazeOWL settings by category)

6. Filter out brands with Logos (automatic default setting)

Warning, terminology overload ahead: The BSR number is the term used to describe how well a product is selling. Both Amazeowl and Jungle Scout use this number for searches. The lower the BSR number, the more units are being sold.

There is not just one BSR number for all of Amazon. **BSR numbers are specific to a given category** (like doll clothes). A BSR of 50,000 may be good for some categories, but terrible for others.

You will learn what an acceptable BSR number is for the type of product you are researching after a few searches. Note: later in the book you will find software products that convert the BSR number to units sold per month, but they still use the same Amazon BSR data as their source.

3.   Jungle Scout Initial Search Criteria

Jungle Scout search criteria include the first 5 items above plus two additional ones.

1.   Star ratings (out of 5 possible)

2.   Quality of the product's Amazon listing (on a zero to 100 scale)

Even though you are not automatically filtering-out brands with logos with Jungle Scout, you should do so manually as you evaluate your results. Conversely, with Amazeowl, **filter out those with 5-star reviews** because you are looking for products that need improvements (so that yours will be better). At the same time highlight those with lower star ratings because they could prove very promising.

While the listing quality is an important metric, you will need to do more research on this issue when you have a short list of competitors in your market niche. Consequently, I do not give much weight to the Jungle Scout number this early in the search process but do consider this when you begin to evaluate your competition.

Spend the time needed with Amazeowl or Jungle Scout to become familiar with the mechanics of using that product. If you do decide to use other paid products later, you will likely find many similarities so that your time will not have been wasted. Note: this is also the time to add columns to your spreadsheet to record those product details that meet your criteria.

4.   Products to be Excluded

The lists from both Jungle Scout and Amazeowl will contain some products that you should not consider. Remove products from further consideration that will be extremely difficult to source or sell. In summary:

- **Filter out brands with Logos** (automatic default setting) because you will not be allowed to sell many of them. This topic requires more time than I am willing to spend for a complete explanation, but for now, do not spend the time to explore selling brand products.

- I would advise against **"complicated" products** and those with many moving parts. Those parts can break and result in poor reviews and increased returns.

- Populate your first cut list with products that are simple, easily understood, and do not require instructions on how to use or maintain. The customer should **understand how to use the product just by looking at a picture**.

- Do not **consider products that come in many different sizes**, colors or other option. The inventory costs quickly get out of control.

- Do not consider **fragile items** that could easily break in transit; this will drive up your returns.

B. Creating a Short List of Products

You should have a reasonable list of products remaining from your searches after excluding those above. You want a reasonable number to ensure that you will have choices available as you continue to gather data, but not so many that it becomes too labor intensive to continue your analysis. Modify your search criteria to adjust for any imbalance, and you might do that any way to further get a feel for the sensitivity of your search criteria at this point.

Next, you need to confirm that you can source this product and find an estimated cost. The Amazeowl software can help with that without contact suppliers directly.

1. Can You Source from Alibaba?

I use the **"Tracked Products" data from Amazeowl** to find both. Even if I created my first list using Jungle Scout, I then turn to Tracked Products to complete the analysis because this free platform provides so much information with just a few clicks. I know that you will need to be familiar with the YT videos about Amazeowl to take full advantage of this section, but this is at the heart of finding your private label product.

Begin your search on Amazeowl by finding a search term that describes your product and your niche. A term that is too broad will return far more products, mostly not relevant to what your customers really want to buy.

To find more relevant products for your customer, try adding specific identifiers to narrow your search and show products only within your niche: identifiers such as the way the product would be used or the materials used to make the product. Just like with your product, if you cannot find a simple search term that "everyone would use" to describe your product niche, then neither will your customers.

You will be able to search Alibaba suppliers for this generic product anonymously, without sending out a request for quote. You will see pictures of similar products that correspond to your search term. If you are disappointed in these products, change your search term to find more appropriate search results.

2. Estimating Your Product Cost

From your search above, you will see estimated cost ranges by each supplier and their offerings. Those costs vary depending on the quantity purchased. You will also find MOQ (Minimum Order Quantity) for each product by the supplier. This will allow you to estimate a range of MOQs and a range of estimated costs for your spreadsheet.

You could click "save," and the average estimate cost will appear in your Amazeowl Tracking data sheet. I suggest that the cost and MOQs of selected products closer to your product, not this average cost, will be more meaningful. From these cost numbers and MOQs on your spreadsheet, you should begin to **estimate your costs and profits**.

Products will continue to be eliminated, or reduced to second-tier consideration and you will constantly be adjusting these estimates with additional data. When done properly, **this spreadsheet should evolve into your business plan** where all your future steps are shown along with cash flows.

I continue to talk about your spreadsheet, but I do not provide an example. Creating your spreadsheet is a big part of what you need to do because it is specific to your needs, and it forces you to consider which elements are important and that you will want later. That is what successful entrepreneurs do.

C. Finding Product Improvements

All the products on your list can be made better with improvements. We know that because you removed any with 5-star reviews. These products sell well but can be improved, so that is where we begin.

Fortunately, you have dozens of former customers who have done the quality assessments for you and have provided you with the detail needed to improve each product. By reading those reviews carefully, you will learn about the quality defects that need to be corrected.

These **reviewers will tell** you specifically about the seams that come apart, the parts missing from the box, scratchy fabric, poor packaging, and so much more. The solution to most of these quality problems will be obvious and easily correctable. If the solutions are not obvious, do not try and reinvent the product, move on to the next one on your list.

I remember searching a product where one of their main bullet points was that they listened to their customers and revised their product, making it heavier with more substantial corners so that it will lie flat and not curl up on the ends. This is the type of quality defect you are searching for when reading reviews, but one that has not already been improved.

Add your findings to your spreadsheet so you can evaluate the specific improvements that you can easily make when talking to your manufacturer. You are beginning to find elements that will appear in your supplier conversations so document them carefully. You might want to even copy and paste some of the reviews you find.

D. Your Best Potential PL Product

You now have a list of products that should sell well and be better than the competition. No doubt one of those products will "jump out at you." It will have a much better ROI, or sales volume, or some other characteristic that grabs your attention and screams "let's go." That is the product idea to carry through the next chapter because you need a product in mind to visualize those steps.

You should then keep these visuals in mind as you complete the study of those concepts found in subsequent chapters. At this point, you will have understood the basics of selling a PL on Amazon. However, I have added a final chapter on selecting your first product to include more detailed analysis on analyzing your competition.

While this is needed to give you the best opportunity for success, I wanted to wait until you understood the entire process and yet knew that your litmus paper was still blue before presenting what could be a tedious chapter for some on this in-depth analysis.

Perhaps your initial product idea will not change after reading this last chapter, but if it does, you have several backup ideas. The reality is that your first choice was made without knowing all the relevant issues. You could start over in the selection process or just start with your short list (recommended), but regardless, the choice of your first PL product should be much better for taking this iterative approach and confirming your choice.

CHAPTER 6. YOUR PRIVATE LABEL PRODUCT: BEST IN CLASS

Y ou completed the last chapter with a short list of products that met your criteria and could be sourced at a profit-generating cost. However, these were almost generic products, before your improvements and further enhancements that will make them the best in class. These enhancements are available to you because you will have a private label.

Substantial value can be added to your product. You are protecting your property by making it more difficult for others to copy, and you will further protect it by having your supplier not sell your labeled product to others because that will be written in your contract (discussed later).

Some people will pay more for a shirt with a recognized symbol on it than the same shirt without that symbol. Among other reasons, the buyer often associates quality with that symbol.

Through your "branding" practices below, you are adding this value of quality for your buyers as well. Do not let them down, because they are paying you to provide that quality consistently on all your products with your product name and logo.

A. Elements of a Private Label

The effort so far to find a private label has been work, intense, detailed, and technical. We need a break, so let's discuss some "right brain" activities. We will discuss adding value to your products for you and your customers.

1. Selecting a Product Name

Invite a friend or spouse to help you brainstorm some ideas, specifically selecting a name for your product. Do not prejudge any suggestion, add every suggestion to your notepad or easel, and then later discuss the merits of each with an open mind. You can make your final decisions later after your brain trust has finished their wine and gone home.

In addition to selecting a product name, also **select an "emotion"** that can be identified with that. Customers buy on emotion. Most customers use facts to reinforce decisions that have already been made on an emotional level.

The sooner you can engender this emotion with a customer, the quicker you get them from "just looking" to "buying." Often your product name is the first word shown above your Title on the listing page, or sometimes among the first words in your Title. Make your product name part of the selling process.

You want to select a product name that conveys the perceived nature of your product line. By this, I am trying to suggest that you want your customer to see your product name and think "fun" if that is one of your themes. But if you are selling a product for a more somber or serious need, you need a product name that projects the idea of a serious nature.

Consider the emotion that you want the customer to feel when they see your product name. The word that elicits a similar emotion in most of your friends is one to include in your list of candidates. Several, similar words also invoke similar emotions, so make liberal use of the thesaurus during your search and expand this list of potential candidates as much as possible.

Your first product may only be the first in what could ultimately be a much larger offering. Therefore, do not limit your product name to only one small segment of markets. Be as expansive as possible, but not so broad as to lose the relationship to your first product.

Consider that if you decide to project "durability" with the name of your product line, there are so many products that you can include under that durability banner. A Product name like "SteelWorks," or so many other similar product names, could be used across very different product lines.

I'll bet you can think of dozens of diverse products that would sell under that product name. You could sell SteelWorks dog chew toys, SteelWorks bicycle products, SteelWorks products for the kitchen.

Here is another approach for your wine drinking group to consider. If someone can identify a competitor, or just a company that they like because of its name, turn again to the thesaurus and kick around some words that work for your group.

Either now or later, you can expand this base product name to include broader headings, like "SteelWorks Environmentally Friendly cat toy" or "SteelWorks Work

Saver utensil." There are phrases like Environmentally Friendly or Work Saver that are both descriptive and emotional, that can be used to further define your product name and elicit additional emotions.

You want all the positive emotions possible when selling. Apple® likely would not have sold as many phones if it had been called "Stevie's Phone Company." So why does your brain-trust on branding think Apple was such a successful name?

2. Designing your logo

The logo will hopefully make that emotion you just created with your product name, develop instantly and fully within your customer when they see it. Well, that is the hope and the desired outcome.

Your wine party quests may include someone with artistic talents capable of creating an image that engenders the emotions you want. This image should be one of your greatest selling tools.

If you and your friends, like me, have zero creative ability, there are low-cost alternatives. If you are not sure what fonts, colors, related pictures, and other features to include in this creative process.

The solution is to use Fiverr or Upwork to find graphic designers. You will find both online, along with many others, capable of doing well those things that you and I do not do well, and doing them at a very reasonable cost.

My experiences with Fiverr work products have been especially impressive, and cheap. Offer to **pay these designers about $5 to $20**, and tip them if they do a good job. Yes, you will likely be very pleasantly surprised at the quality of their work.

Once you have acceptable logos, solicit the opinion of others and see what the consensus is. The final decision is yours, but if no one else likes your choice of names or logos, you might want to have another wine party and invest another $20 in logo designs.

Technical notes: You will want the logo in a file type that can be used later to send to the printer to make those labels. Also, you will want the logo in a file that permits revisions, and you will want the logo in a file that is easy for you to use.

If you have already addressed placing your logo directly on your product, you should have a file type used by your manufacturer for this purpose. These are different file types that you can discuss with your designer.

I understand that these issues may seem confusing, but your designer will be familiar with these concepts and help you make those decisions. They do this routinely.

You do not need to learn extensively about the various file types, just note how they can be used. I know that I have already belabored the file type issue well beyond just being tedious.

My further point is that you do not need to know the technical details of this or most other issues, because you can have someone who does know this well to work on this for you. You should expect that it will become second nature for you to turn to the virtual community after you have experienced the ease of using these talented individuals.

3. Package Decisions

Your package needs to be visually appealing, but that does not necessarily mean expensive. You may want to design a very specific package that reflects your uniquely designed product at some point, and I would recommend that you do that. For your first order, you could also just use a plain white box which most suppliers have available.

To provide information about what your product name should convey to customers, consider painting a picture of the emotions you want with a "sticker" on your first product box. Use the **logo and product name created by your online service** printed on an attractive sticker. If this is the case, tell the designers, as they create project files, to also provide you with the correct file type for that purpose.

Later, you can pay for the design directly on product boxes when that makes dollar sense. This could be more important when you are selling beyond just the Amazon marketplace.

Note: If you intend to print your designs directly onto a box to, then you will need to have the manufacturer send you the box template for the designers to use. The online designers can do this as well.

Your requirements also include placing the country of origin on the package and your company contact information. You will find Amazon general packaging requirements on Sellers Central. Ask your supplier for any other requirements specific to your product that he may have addressed before.

B. Branding Your Product

The Amazon requirements for being a Branded product were changed in 2017 and are much more demanding. Among other requirements, you will now **need a registered trademark.** Those with that Branded status prior to these changes were grandfathered in, but you and I were not.

I do recommend that you consider becoming a Branded product, but your first product will not likely qualify initially. However, because of your Private Label, you will be selling a brand as far as your customers are concerned whether officially Branded at Amazon or not.

There are advantages, special benefits, available to Branded products at Amazon. In the future, you also may want to move into additional marketplaces to augment your Amazon sales. For this and other reasons, it is worth considering obtaining a U. S. registered trademark.

1. Trademarking Your product

Using your Name and logo, selling products where both appear on your packaging and with your logo appearing on your product itself will enhance your ability to get a TM (Trademark) later. I do recommend that you do this with all your private label products, starting with the first one whether you officially apply for a TM or not.

To register as a Brand Owner at Amazon, there must be a U. S. registered TM on your product. That allows you to **legally place the ® symbol** on your product after your name and logo.

You may be able to register with Amazon if you can show that you have a TM pending. Amazon will accept the pending serial number by showing that you have begun the registration process with USPTO (US Patent and Trade Office). You cannot use the ® during the time your application is pending.

The USPTO procedure is tedious, and the cost is currently $275 per class of product. After you submit your application, an attorney will be assigned, and you will need to follow up with him periodically so that your application does not "go dormant."

It is not unusual for this process to take a year or longer. If you decide to become an Amazon Brand Owner, you will need to begin the process well in advance.

The use of a trademark can sometimes be a deterrent to others copying your design. If you believe this might help your product, pay the filing fee with USPTO to legally use "TM" on your first product and advance the branding process. There is little downside to taking this approach from a business perspective.

2. Enhance Brand Content

Once you have completed the Branding process, you can consider applying for EBC (Enhanced Brand Content). The primary benefits are:
- Enhanced design features available on your listing page

- Adding videos to your listing page

- Enhanced "Sponsored Products" promotions which lead to:

o   More views when customers search

o   More targeted keywords

Amazon offers these benefits at a price. Depending on the category of your product, you will pay another 5% to the standard 6-15% sales fee.

You are not likely to place your brand into the EBC program anytime soon. I bring this up as an example of what may be available to you later, but primarily to give you an idea of advantages that well-established competitors have over your new product.

When you are searching for your product niche, consider those with videos, and many reviews, and do not include them in your niche initially. However, joining that elite group should be one of your long-term considerations.

3.   Competing against EBC Listings

This is not a scientific survey on the **advantages of having an EBC Listing**, but I looked at three very similar toys with and without videos in December 2017. Those with videos were selling at $4 to $7 higher and with significantly more sales. If substantiated, these increased Buy Box prices and sales would more than justify the additional 5%.

This isolated example may have given completely erroneous results compared to a better survey. I would not argue otherwise, but it is enough for me to be curious about whether this program might be beneficial for my product.

Later, after you have a successful product, discuss TM and EBC with Amazon to find some current, more comprehensive data specific to your product niche. These programs will be a year old by spring 2018, and these data will be available.

C.   Providing Extras

One of the best ways to differentiate your product from others, to enhance its perceived value, and to improve your customer's experience is **by including a small complementary item** in your product package. If you are selling a baby wrap, include a headband made of the same material as a free accessory. If you are selling a pet product for $25-$30, include one of the many available small, inexpensive pet products that a pet owner would also use.

I am going to refer you to Kole Imports, just one of many online distributors of inexpensive products where you can find such items for way under one dollar. Pick a hypothetical product and go through their catalog with the ideas of finding an inexpensive way to enhance that product. This exercise should also help you with ideas when you deal with your supplier.

If your product has a small part that can easily be lost, get your supplier to include an extra. If there is a replaceable part that may be needed in a short to interim time period, include one in your package.

Many of these add-on value items can be included by your supplier for free or for very little additional cost. You are trying to make your product stand out from your competition.

As part of your search for a product that you can improve, you will likely find several suggestions while reading your competitors' reviews. In the process of adding perceived value, and improving on your competitors' products, you also allow yourself to increase the selling price.

Adding a couple of dollars to your price along with added sales is a terrific incentive to consider adding extras. Do not overlook this terrific sales incentive; work at making this happen.

D. Selling as a Gift?

If you have a product that can reasonably be sold as a gift, you may want to advertise it as such. The option to have Amazon gift wrap it is available.

One point to remember is that as an FBA seller, you turn over all the management of your inventory to Amazon. This includes gift wrapping.

Amazon will charge the buyer, credit you with that charge, and then immediately debit your account for the same amount. The cost is, therefore, a "wash" for the seller, Amazon profits from the wrapping. Knowing this should also help you better understand the sales reports which show this charge being both debited and credited to your account.

If you have enabled the gift wrapping option through your Seller Central account, you can also allow the buyer to include a gift message. Consider this option for two reasons; not only might there be additional sales, but this might **also reduce your returns**. Gifts are much less likely to be returned compared to other sales.

The mechanics are: Sellers Central> Settings > Gift Options> Edit next to Gift Wrap or Gift-Wrap and enable service for each item> Continue to save these setting. To disallow this option in the future: Sellers Central> Settings > Gift Options> "Remove" (permanently) or "Disable" (temporarily) next to the gift option no longer available.

CHAPTER 7. FINDING A RELIABLE SUPPLIER

W ithin the global economy, countries have developed specialties for which they are particularly well suited. Some have natural resources which they export.

Individual companies have developed intellectual products and have become exporters from several different regions and countries where the supply of human talent exists. China has used sections of their vast lands to build modern factories where they employ talented individuals for wages less than many of their competitors.

A. Using Alibaba to find a supplier

Now that Alibaba has been developed, anyone can access thousands of these manufacturers directly to manufacture their products. There is now one platform online that provides some level of security, and a list of suppliers that meet their quality standards along with catalogs to make our job of sourcing easy.

There are other platforms, and other countries available. However, the Alibaba platform has developed ahead of their competitors and makes this the one for the novice to explore first.

Go to Alibaba.com and sign up for an account. Begin to explore their site by entering a phrase that describes your product of interest.

As potential suppliers appear, look at information about the company and their products. The site will quickly become intuitive to use.

You are advised to use the Alibaba site to correspond with these suppliers initially. After you establish a corresponding relationship, you may find that using your business email account is more convenient.

Tip: I make it a practice to **create a new email account**. You can do this easily just by adding a number (or product word) after your core email address. You will need to do this to isolate the many responses that you are likely to get from just one inquiry.

B. Contacting suppliers with RFQ

You should **select 10 to 15 potential suppliers** from the Alibaba catalogs online. Your first list should include those with experience manufacturing your product line and exporting to your country. Eliminate those who fail to meet the criteria below.

- First, consider those with the Gold Star and look at the number of years as shown on Alibaba. This does not tell you a great deal, but you want to deal with a supplier who is large enough and has several years of experience.

  This is a reasonable start to reducing the large number of potential suppliers. The Sponsored Listings means only that they have paid to have their names on this list; it does not refer to a recommendation, so ignore this list.

- Look at their catalogs to see if they make related products and the number and complexity of these related products. The pictures are a quick way to see if there might be a fit for your needs. You do not want to contact someone who has just one bicycle seat for sale and many more ceramic items.

- Look at the company link to see the countries they supply. You want to see North America, and perhaps Europe or Australia included.

  Stay away from those servicing only Asia and other areas where the quality standards and importing requirements are likely to be very different. While this may be your first time to import, you do not want this to be the first time for your manufacturer to export to your country.

1. Your initial contact with suppliers

I am going to provide a template for the first contact letter you should send as your RFQ (Request For Quote). (See below.) You are trying to develop a relationship with them, so start by telling them about your company and how they can benefit from being your supplier.

You are entering a **business culture of "Guanxi,"** a Chinese term that roughly translates into networks or connections. But the expectations are for a far more mutually beneficial arrangement that includes trust, support, and cooperation by both parties.

You are small now, but you expect to grow and become a more valuable buyer of their products. You are going to take a direct business approach to this relationship while building trust.

You need to be honest and do not pretend to be someone other than who you are. For example, you do not need a "more professional" business email address; your Gmail account will do fine.

The supplier wants to deal with a **knowledgeable buyer**, someone who can express exactly what they want. Convey that attitude in your initial contact with a well-constructed RFQ.

Spend the necessary time to build your **product specifications so that it is all-inclusive**. You do not want to surprise someone later with a requirement that you forgot to include.

There will be reasonable modifications needed as you discuss the manufacturing details with your supplier, and you need to indicate your flexibility on these matters. Take advantage of his expertise in manufacturing while you exercise your developing expertise in product sourcing and online selling.

2. RFQ Template

My name is Jason Beaver from American Buy N Ride Products. We are a small online seller, expecting to grow over the next nine months.

We are looking to source a bicycle seat cover for sale in the US market; see our specifications below. We will need to develop a relationship with a manufacturer to meet our mutual needs.

Our product goal is to sell a unique bicycle seat cover that is both very comfortable, attractive and durable. Our sales goal is to sell 5,000 to 10,000 pcs annually.

Our initial order will be for your MOQ of 500 seats to test market this bicycle seat in our online distribution chain and get customer feedback. From your Alibaba postings, you seem to produce a seat cover similar to the one we will be selling. Are you interested in producing a sample to our specifications?

Product Specifications: Size (inches and cm), material, quality, color, etc. that would completely identify your product. Include any comments about why a specific item is included in your specification. Make special note of those specifications you have chosen to add value to your product that may be different from your competitors.

Product Packaging: Please send the box specifications for those you normally use. We will want our package design to be included later; however, we will use a plain box for our test order.

Can you add a self-adhesive logo "stickers" to each product package for our first order? We can provide these to your manufacturing site.

[Note: **Include questions about their abilities.**]

1. Are you a manufacturer or trading company? [Note: either is acceptable, but you want to know if there might be delays in the decision chain from a trading company to his manufacturer. There could also be advantages in that the trading company could have access to more manufacturers that you see on Alibaba.

2. Are you familiar with the materials in our specifications, and have you used them in seats? [Note: you may not be the first to see the advantages in making the product changes that you identified reading the reviews, and someone may already have "your product" available.]

3. What is your lead time for the samples and the order? [Note: these are important to your decision lines for launching your new product and for managing your inventory to ensure that you do not run out.]

4. Can we add our logo to the seat, and if so, where can it be added? [Note: you will want your logo to be an integral part of the product if possible. You also want your logo on your packaging as you grow your product lines and begin advertising.]

5. What is the sample cost and shipping by express to the US? [Note: your sample will be delivered by air, but your first order may be shipped by sea, depending on the product size and weight.]

Thank you for your reply.
Jason Beaver
American Buy N Ride Products

3. Evaluating potential suppliers

You need to evaluate your needs and the ability of these potential suppliers at this early stage to find the one(s) with whom you want to develop a relationship.

Eventually, you **will want more than one supplier** to ensure that your supply chain is durable and capable of withstanding unforeseen difficulties later.

Initially, you must objectively, and quickly, drop those who do not measure up to your needs. You can expect that a high percentage of your RFQs will respond.

- You will need to discuss details of your sample and your order with this supplier. Communication is one of the most important characteristics to be comfortable with at this early stage.

   Are you comfortable with their English? Do they respond quickly to your follow up questions?

- "Wechat" and "Skype" are common live communications apps in China. Using them will dramatically shorten and improve the process of establishing trust and answering questions that will arise.

   Consider using these tools after you are down to your shortlist and make your final decision to answer your questions about communications better. They will also be great tools for resolving the many detail questions each of you will have before you can place your first order.

- Do they seem willing to work with your product needs, and do their follow up questions indicate knowledge of your product concept?

- Did they give you confidence in their ability to produce the product you want? Do they have experience working with the materials and product concept laid out in your specifications? Did they provide additional insight into the manufacturing process that was helpful?

- If you are down to 2 or 3 that seem acceptable, make your final decision, but do not burn any bridges with the others. You may need a backup if your first choice does not work out, and later when you are trying to add another backup supplier to make your supply chain more robust.

4. Ordering samples

After finalizing what your product will be as produced by your manufacturer, the production specifications need to be documented precisely so that both parties have the same understanding. You may have discussed other, even future, modifications (including different materials and quality standards) along the way to reaching this point, and you do not want any misunderstanding to cause a problem with your first production sample.

You expect that the sample will be representative of the first production run. You will want some level of **manufacturer's quality inspection** for the first production run, probably pictures from several angles to include the packaging. Use the same procedure for this sample, so that the production run pictures go smoothly.

You will **need to pay for a sample** to be produced and shipped in advance. Many manufacturers today will accept Paypal.

There is a fee of about 3% associated with using Paypal, but this and all other costs should be included in your sample charge. Do not expect to use your credit card.

5. Supplier Pictures and Quality Control Issues

You now have the sample in its package and can check for the quality and details you were expecting. The pictures taken by your supplier were a good indication of what you received, and there were no surprises.

Do you have confidence that this is all the quality control you will need for your first order? If you do not have a product with moving parts, then a picture taken by your supplier may be all you need to authorize shipment when your first order is ready.

You ultimately want the product to go directly from your supplier to the Amazon warehouses. Your packaging should meet the Amazon requirements, including applying the code number by which your product will be known to Amazon. That number will likely be the ASIN code (Amazon Standard Identification Number) codes.

I would recommend this code be applied before shipment, but you can have Amazon apply the ASIN codes for you at a cost of 20 cents each. However, you must be confident that your order is right in every detail before sending it to Amazon.

If your investment is comparatively large, and you do not have confidence that your supplier's pictures alone will provide the needed quality assurance, you have an alternative. You might want to hire a service based in China to make an onsite inspection.

They will send you the report before you authorize the final payment. The cost should be several hundred dollars, but a small amount compared to the total amount at risk. **This is a judgment call** that only you can make.

6. Shipping Decisions to Amazon

Air shipments will be more expensive than shipping by sea, but you may be willing to pay the difference to shorten your supply chain and better control inventory and inventory costs. Remember that Amazon does charge you monthly for their inventory space.

I am presenting a **"rule of thumb" table** to compare different shipping modes. As you know, rules of thumb are notoriously imprecise, but they do indicate relative orders of magnitude.

I use kilograms rather than pounds because this is generally used in international trade. Note: you should also try to communicate your quantitative factors in metric units when dealing with your supplier to avoid confusion.

Weight- Mode	Delivery Time	Costs
<50 kg – Air Currier	3–5 Days	$7 / kg
<500 kg – Air Freight	7–10 Days	$5 / kg
>500 kg – Ocean Freight	30–40 Days	$0.60 / kg

You can ask your supplier to handle the shipment of your product directly to Amazon, or to your home/facility if that was your earlier decision. The alternative is for you to handle this yourself, and you may be able to save costs (in the future) by doing so.

If your supplier handles all shipment issues, inquire about how duties and fees are to be paid. Your supplier needs to set up communications for you on these costs.

I would suggest that eventually (perhaps not for your first order), you Google an air/sea freight forwarder and contact one to learn about their process. By doing this, you will have several different service providers and shippers bidding for your business which should reduce your costs.

Tip: the Freightos.com site is one that has been recommended because the process is easy for beginners, and the support staff is friendly and helpful. Eventually, you will want to do this yourself, and you have time after ordering the sample and before it arrives to do this.

You will need the specifics on the number of cartons, size and weight, shipping locations (ports and zip codes in the US) and dates for your first order. There is also an HTS number (Harmonized Tariff Schedule code number) that is used to help specify the appropriate import regulations and tariffs involved for your specific product.

Your supplier can provide the HTS number as well as the other data needed. Collect this information because you will need it later.

Similarly, the freight forwarder's staff should help you on other decisions you will need to make, but the process should not be intimidating. You just want to learn how to use the freight forwarders, not become an expert in the many aspects of importing.

This is just another skill set you will develop as part of your product sourcing responsibilities. However, with all that is involved in your first order, let the supplier handle this initially.

C. Placing your first order

You now have your acceptable sample; you have discussed the confidential nature of your product and the exclusivity of your product. Now you can negotiate the MOQ, rates, and terms for your first order.

However, you should also negotiate the second order after you have reached an accommodation with terms and conditions for the first order. This is where your true leverage exists.

1. Negotiating the First and Second Orders

You have begun the "Guanxi" relationship we discussed earlier, and now it is time to absolutely nail-down all money-related issues previously discussed with your supplier. You get confirmation for his MOQ and his FOB or EXW prices, and his delivered prices to Amazon, now that all details have been concluded.

You should be asking these questions along the way as you discuss changes. Now, you should receive clarifications if there are any doubts about the costs.

You could take your work to date and go to other suppliers and ask them to bid for comparison, and you might save a little, or maybe not. However, you would hurt the relationship that you worked to build.

Instead, work with these numbers. If something seems out of line with expectations, discuss it, and work it out to your mutual satisfaction.

Your objective is not to save a little on the first order. You want a reliable partner who will help when the unforeseen happens.

You should have priced in your expectations for all costs as you went forward with this process and you should have a reasonable profit in mind. Do not screw up this relationship for a few pennies.

Take a little less profit on this first order, if necessary, but negotiate the next order now. Get a break based on a larger second order, so **negotiate a schedule for higher order quantities** into the foreseeable future.

2. Pro Forma Invoice

Ask your supplier to send you a Pro Forma Invoice. This is where you can add the terms and conditions that you have discussed as you reached this point in the process.

Add the specifications you agreed upon, the quality assurance process you intend to use (self-inspect pictures, or outside inspection report). Include the shipping dates and the shipping details that the supplier is to handle along with the MOQ and price.

Note: prices are generally quoted FOB (Free-On-Board, at the shipping port) if you are shipping by sea and EXW (Ex-Works) if you are shipping by air. You will **use this Pro Forma Invoice as your contract.**

3. Paying for your Order

You should expect to pay with a bank transfer of funds. One of the terms and conditions of your Pro Forma Invoice should include that you will pay a percentage of the order up front, and the remainder after the pictures and outside quality report you receive are accepted.

If you agree to a 30% down and 70% before shipment, this would be expressed as 30/70 TT. A down payment of up to 50% would be common when you are making changes in the supplier's stock items.

Your supplier will provide the details of his bank account so that you can arrange with your bank to make the transfer of the down payment. Do check the supplier bank details to confirm they agree with your information from Alibaba.

No mistrust or disrespect is being shown here; this is just **good business practice**.

If the supplier requests a **Western Union funds transfer, STOP**; this is a red flag. If you do this, there is a significant chance that you will lose your money and have very limited recourse.

CHAPTER 8. LISTING YOUR PRODUCT ON AMAZON

Whon customers search for a product like yours and then decide to click on your specific product, this is the page they will see. Your Listing is **how your customer will learn about your product**, and you will either sell your product or lose a sale according to their response to this page.

I cannot overemphasize the importance of this sales tool. This is worthy of intense attention initially where you will put everything you have learned to create the best listing possible.

You will also return to this repeatedly as you learn more and you experiment to see what is working. Getting better at this process is your goal for each new product.

A.   Keywords, SERPS, and Your Listing

To get a customer to your Listing page, you need to create keywords that will show your page as one of the options on the first page of the **SERP (Search Engine Return Pages)**. If a customer were to search for "comfortable bicycle seat," then your product needs to pop up on that first page of options. Most of the sales for comfortable bicycle seat will come from that page. Understanding how the Amazon algorithm works will help you to do well with the SERP.

1.   The Amazon A9 Algorithm

The Amazon A9 algorithm itself is proprietary, but we do know some things about how it works. It **ranks products by their "Relevancy."** While relevancy is defined by the algorithm, Amazon has said that one way to improve the ranking is to use the most relevant keywords in your title, bullets, and description.

Several software products help understand the relative importance of certain KWs (KeyWords). Keyword Planner (a free tool if you open an Adword account on Google) is useful for KW searches in Google.

KW Inspector (paid software you may need if you use Amazeowl for product searches) is a tool for analyzing KWs in Amazon searches. An argument can be made that KW Inspector is more relevant for your purposes, but initially you can get a good idea of what works on Google for free, and generally, there is often a correlation between the two.

One additional free KW product I like is TheHoth. You can also use these tools to see where competitors' KWs show up in SERPs, and this is where I would start to create the keywords for my Listing.

Run the titles of your competitors to rank their performance, but also to see what has been working for them. You want to improve on your competitors' Listings, but also to learn from the better ones.

Generally, I have found that the more successful competitors have also found the best KWs. You do not need to reinvent the wheel, just find out which wheels roll the fastest and catch a ride.

There are four areas within your listing that Amazon uses to find keywords for their search engine. The only actual comprehensive study of this issue that I have seen concluded that the most important location, by far, was the Title.

I give significant weight to studies like this that contain their data along with their results and conclusions. Most information on this subject seems to be opinion pieces, and not objectively data-based. KWs in any of the other locations (Bullets, Description, and Backend) were much less beneficial.

2.   The Title

The Title is not simply a collection of KWs; however, the Title will also be read by a machine so the clever entrepreneur will find a way to weave those KWs into direct, easily understood phrases. Everyone seems to have their own philosophy of how to write Titles.

My concept is that Titles are read by humans to find a product for which they were searching. The most successful Titles are written for humans, telling them about the product and why it satisfies their needs.

Amazon seems to discourage "delimiters" like commas, hyphens, and slashes, but I believe you can use three or four separate phrases, separated by a delimiter and that helps readability. Mobile users will be helped by using bold, italicized important words, and I do not see a downside to this practice, especially when mobile traffic continues to increase.

The Title can be close to 200 characters long, but only about 110 will be visible on most desktops. Think of this valuable real estate as divided into three or four different sections, each with a specific task to perform.

The first 35 characters, along with a picture, will be used if you decide to run Headline Ads. This should clearly explain your product, leaving no doubt what you are selling.

When reading on your detailed product page, the customer should know they are in the right place following their search and subsequently clicking on your product picture. This is your goal using the first 35 characters although use a few more to do this if you must.

The next title section should sell your product to those who saw your main picture and read your first 35 characters. You should explain how your product solves a problem of theirs or is unique but sell it.

This section in your Title should contain more characters than the others and should convince your readers that this is the product they need. Your product will **satisfy their needs**, solve their problems.

The challenge is to accomplish this with limited characters, so choose your wording carefully with that in mind. Concentrate on needs or uniqueness with words designed to elicit an emotional response and build a desire to purchase.

The last Title section can contain additional keywords, but all set within a "readable" framework. **Do not "stuff keywords"** into this section thinking that no one (only a computer) will read them.

Use this to solve additional problems, but with more emphasis on using any major keywords not used earlier in the first two sections. The location of the KWs within the Title is not important to the A9 algorithm, and remember that you do not need to repeat the same KWs solely to improve the SERP.

Allow me to emphasize that the challenge of writing the Title is to include your high-ranking keywords while at the same time making a reader-friendly case for buying your product. If you must choose between connecting with the customer and adding another keyword, remember that you are trying to get the customer to understand your product and buy it.

You want them to click the Add to Cart Button by solving their problem, not getting a higher search score. Just the opposite, if visitors view your Listing Page, but do not buy, you will **hurt your future SERPs** by the A9 algorithm.

3. Bullets

The bullet points section is where you explain more fully what you mentioned, or would have liked to mention, in your title. Your customer is looking on Amazon to solve a problem or make their lives better.

What problems does your product solve and **how could it make their lives better?** Your product has features that will satisfy these two concerns so tell them how these features will do that in a bullet format. (Note: Simply listing features is not making your Listing the best it can be, yet so many listings do just that.)

This also becomes a "table of contents" for your much more expansive Description. However, many customers will not read the entire Description, and by the time they reach your Bullets, this may be your last opportunity to sell them.

All your emotional words that will drive a purchase (along with your Title and Pictures) need to be covered by the time those 6 Bullets are read. You must sell them by the time they finish reading your bullets; do not think that the Description will make the sale for you.

Write down your competitors' bullets and rate them, then improve upon them. Work with that concept so that it becomes natural for you and you will create better listings than your competitors.

Much of what you will do in your Listing is to rate and improve upon your competitors' efforts that preceded your attempt to create the best product and sell it more effectively. You have the advantage of using their efforts so take full advantage of that. Your work will go faster, and you will have a better result.

4. Description

The Description is where you **expand upon your thoughts in the Bullets** to describe in more detail why yours is the product that satisfies the reasons they came to Amazon to search in the first place. You already did the heavy lifting with the thought that went into creating the bullets. You have a maximum of 2,000 characters to complete your appeal and convert the visitor to a customer.

Think about what questions your customers may have that could not be answered fully in the Title or Bullets. Use the Bullets as a guide to frame your Description, but also expand upon those to describe why your product is better than the competitions'.

I want to comment on the process of creating your Listing. The Description allows you to use a conversational tone to sell your products useful attributes, and it may be easier to start with this and then condense these thoughts into Bullets and your Title.

Some find that by writing all three simultaneously helps. Try the different ways to see which works best for you.

5. Backend KW Optimization

Backend optimization **allows you use 1,000 characters in each of 5 fields** to improve search results. You will find this as you continue through the listing process. This is a place for those of you who want to stuff your KW list somewhere.

You will have created a long list of KWs when you analyzed your competition and tried to find KWs on your own. After you have created your Listing, test KW efficiency by randomly selecting from this list and use the Amazon search bar to see if your product is shown in the search ressults. (Note: It may take 24 hours after your listing has been completed for you to try this technique.)

6. Photos

Your Photos will be the first of your sales tools that the customer will see when visiting your Listing. Use a competent service to product them; do not take them yourself with your cell phone camera.

The photos should be a minimum of 1,000 pixels on the long side and 500 on the short side to be "zoomable." I recommend that you specify **1500 by 1500 pixels** with a white background because this presents the best visual image to customers.

You should upload the nine images allowed and experiment with which ones will be the most effective. Unfortunately, you will not be allowed to upload videos in the beginning; this is reserved for those with Enhanced Content privileges, which you should strive for in the future.

This is **one of the most important sales tools** you have. The customer cannot touch or "handle" your product, but these six photos are the best equivalent connection that you have. The written word is important, but most of your customers will be impacted more by your product images.

Like all other sales tools, **use an emotional element** when designing them for your photographer. Use images of someone using it, holding it or unwrapping it.

The cost of photos does not need to be expensive. Use a virtual photographer from Upwork, Fiverr or some other online source. You should expect a first-class job, to your specifications for not much money.

B. More About KW Relevancy and the A9 Algorithm

More work is ahead; your listing efforts are just the first step to producing a better SERP. **You also need a good sales history**. The A9 algorithm uses several factors in defining relevancy, including:

- o Click-through rates (page views), the rate at which customers clicked through to see your Listing page following their SERP.

- o Conversion rates, the rate at which customers purchased your product after viewing your page.

- o Sales, meaning how many units have you sold.

- o Product price currently compared to your competitors.

The guiding principle for A9 is to provide the most relevant results and lowest prices to potential customers for their product searches. To do this, the algorithm monitors the KWs searched, which products were clicked for further review, and which product was ultimately purchased.

1. The Most Important SERP Factor

The most important SERP factor is the **sales history for a specific KW search term**, and by extension, sales resulting from a search of the KWs in your Title. Not to preach, but **please reread that last sentence** and understand how important that concept is to your business. **Converting search terms into sales is** the most important factor in raising you to the top of the SERP results.

I discussed the practice of some sellers to stuff their titles with KWs designed to bring customers to their page, hoping that someone looking for a very marginally relevant product will buy theirs. For example, someone might decide to use "baby shower gift" as a keyword for a rug designed for a child's room.

Because your child's room rug was not what they expected to see, even though one or two might buy, this practice will reduce your conversion rate for that KW. Reducing your KW conversion rate will significantly hurt your SERP.

Do not use KWs that will draw clicks, but not result in sales. OK, I am preaching, but this is an all-too-common mistake made by beginners.

2. Using Price to Improve SERP

One often overlooked element that you can control in improving your SERP is the Price. Setting your prices below market averages can boost three important factors, page views, conversions, and orders. You can start high, then reduce the price, and see benefits in these three factors.

Dropping the Price can bring a dramatic increase in sales. **Do this slowly,** collecting data, to ensure that you do not suddenly run out of inventory.

Market data suggests that if you subsequently increase prices (other than in exceptional market conditions), you will hurt all three factors:

- Click-through rates,

- Conversion rates

- Sales history

It will often be very difficult to restore these three factors simply by reducing prices again to the original level. To increase sales again, you may need other optimizing actions, improving your Listing or increased Promotions (discussed in Chapter 9 on Promoting Your Product).

CHAPTER 9. PROMOTING YOUR PRODUCT

P romoting your new product is about the effort to bring Amazon traffic to your product page initially at launch, but also about sustaining and increasing traffic over time. The initial effort to launch your product requires time and money.

This effort will increase traffic over the short run, but you need to continue and to expand your efforts. If you are not paying attention to the elements needed to expand your traffic, at some point, your traffic will begin to decline.

For your first product, I believe that the SP-Ads will be all that most new products will need to **start the "flywheel effect."** That is, advertising to get product page "views," leading to sales, leading to improved Sales Ranking status which is used by the A9 algorithm to gain higher visibility by SERP, and back to page views.

Hence the ever-increasing flywheel effect as your sales metrics improve with each cycle. However, there are also techniques that can be used later, and by those with more experience, to drive traffic to your product page with traffic originating from outside the Amazon platform.

For your first product launch, concentrate on SP-Ads. Rather than covering that subject here, I have provided a separate chapter (12) on Outside Traffic for that purpose.

A. Initial Launch of Your New Product

You have your Listing, and you paid close attention to the KWs, photos and other elements needed to make this Listing (and your product) better than your

competition. Your product is listed in the largest online catalog, and Amazon will bring millions of customers to this catalog.

Your next task is to ensure that the A9 algorithm that you worked so hard to accommodate with your product listing is working for you. You need A9 to bring you customers so they can buy, but A9 only shows customers those products with high conversion rates and a history or sales.

How do we solve this vexing conundrum? This is a classic "chicken and the egg" problem.

The solution is to advertise with the built-in PPC (Pay Per Click equivalent for Google) option called Sponsored Products Ads on Amazon. This is the one skill set needed by the new seller for a successful launch designed to improve your SERP and overcome the chicken-egg conundrum.

I discussed "learning your craft" and its importance. A part of this learning is to practice and experiment with the SP-Ads (Sponsored Products Ads) campaign during your first product launch so that you are comfortable with using this.

You also need to budget for this while you are creating your spreadsheet to understand how these ads will impact your profits. If you cannot afford these costs, then you have the wrong price structure.

As an estimate for planning purposes, consider 20-40% of sales for the first 4 to 6 weeks, dropping to 10-15% as an ongoing, cost. Each product will have its unique issues and improved estimates of advertising costs which will come with experience.

While the discussion will be directed at your product launch, these ads will also be used in the future to drive incremental product sales. Keep this in mind as you read this section.

You will be introduced into the "automatic" campaign initially as described below. Using results from the automatic campaign, you will be using the "manual" campaigns to grow your sales beyond the launch phase.

1. Sponsored Products Ads

You have been introduced to SP-Ads several times as part of previous discussions so let's cover them in more detail. You will see products listed as "Amazon Sponsored Products" that appear prominently after a search.

These are products where the seller paid Amazon to place their listing advantageously when the customers searched for a keyword. They may be placed on the side, top or bottom of a search page.

You just bid on a specific keyword that you believe your customers will use to find your product. If your bid is the highest, your listing will be shown to this potential customer, and you will be charged.

You can **set the maximum amount per day** that you are willing to spend for this service so you can control your spending. You can also select the beginning and ending dates for your campaigns. A week to 10 days should be long enough for this first phase.

You put in a lot of effort to select these KWs would be helpful, but how do you know they will create sales? You find out by using the "automatic option" during this first phase to collect data about the KWs included in your Listing.

While the automatic option will also be used initially to promote your product, the primary objectives are to evaluate the KWs used in your original Listing and to find KWs that are worth bidding on later in a Manual Campaign. You should also consider revising your title listing based on the automatic results (see below).

2. Reports from Automatic Sponsored Product Ads

The concept is to allow the Amazon algorithm to match customer searches to your product by using the automatic option. That is, the KWs located within **the Search Terms used by the customers** to find your product will be the ones that drive them to your product listing.

The words themselves are important, but also the syntax of the Search Terms used by customers impacts results. Customers may use your KWs but what is the surrounding context; what are the surrounding words, the syntax?

By using the automatic campaign, you will find out how to optimize your Listing and create a more cost-effective Manual Campaign. You will be able to do this by analyzing campaign reports from Seller Central.

3. Listing Optimization

This is an ongoing exercise that most successful sellers engage in constantly through 'tweaks" by experimenting and documenting results:

- Which keywords in your listing are working, and others that you may want to bring from your Bullets and Description into your Title.

- The reports may identify KWs used by customers that you did not consider, or did not include in your Listing. These may be KWs that your competition did not use because they did appear very popular in search engines.

    Even with low popularity ratings, they could be very efficient (high conversion rate) at driving sales for those few customers who do use them.

Finding a few customers who use those KWs resulting in high conversions is a win-win-win.

- Identify KWs drawing traffic to your page, but not creating sales. **Traffic that views your page, but does not convert to sales is hurting your SERP** and needs attention. Your competitors' KWs were one source of your original list of potential KWs, as well as data on KWs that were popular, so you included them to drive traffic.

  You may now find that some of these KWs are bringing traffic, but hurting both you and these competitors. You can now improve your competitive position by eliminating them.

  You can also identify which competitors do not understand the value of reports from SP-Ads as you monitor their strengths and weaknesses. All these data go into your spreadsheet.

4. Collecting Data for a Manual Campaign

Data are collected from the automatic campaign for use in designing a Manual Campaign, but data from all campaigns need to be documented for constant revisions to optimize the Manual Campaigns. Be careful not to lose data from a campaign when you update to a more efficient campaign. Once you designate a campaign as "archived," the data can no longer be retrieved.

- Identify KWs that are worthwhile bidding on in your Manual SP-Ads and the estimated costs. Placing a cost to benefit ratio for KWs is the way you design your Manual Campaign for efficiency and will form the basis for your advertising budget.

- You may also identify keywords that are working well, but competitors are not bidding on, and perhaps you can buy these for very little during the next manually targeted words campaign. These should become the bedrock of your ongoing campaigns, but monitor the results to see if these are becoming more expensive as others discover them.

- Some KWs will be too expensive now, but monitor these to see if the bid price drops. You will be able to optimize your Listing by knowing which KWs are working, even if you decide not to bid on them at their current levels.

5. Manual Sponsored Product Ads Campaign

I know that taking this step to pay for advertising can cause you to hesitate, but it is necessary. Take the time to complete a spreadsheet on advertising costs to mentally prepare yourself. Set limits that give you peace of mind that you can afford these costs.

Include the automatic campaign in the spreadsheet to collect data in the first phase, but also include a manually targeted KW campaign at a reasonable funding level for the remainder of the month, and a continuing campaign into the future. You may want to vary these costs to see how this impacts your budget, but give each cost level 10 days to fully see the effects.

Your goal is to make your listing competitive, with constantly improving sales, based on feedback reports from your ad campaign. You will be able to reduce your ACoS (Advertising Cost of Sales) by collecting data during the automatic and the Manual Campaigns.

You will see your conversions improve and your sales increase with a well-constructed launch campaign that includes:

- Paid advertising

- Discounted sales

- An optimized listing

- And soliciting reviews via the emails sent to your customers

You want to learn about the reports available through your Seller Account. You will learn how to more effectively spend these ad dollars based on the data in your campaign reports.

Do not spend ad dollars without knowing the results, and those cost/sales data come from those objective, data-filled reports. The analysis and peace of mind that you are making the right decisions come from your frequently updated spreadsheet.

6. The Mechanics of Creating a Sponsored Product Ad Campaign

You will create your first campaign from your Seller Account. The mechanics of this are Seller Central> Advertising (tab next to Orders)> Campaign Manager (drop-down menu> Create Campaign).

At this point, think about a system of naming campaigns so that each has a unique name that will differentiate it from future campaigns, and will give you the information you will need concerning what this campaign is designed to accomplish. Doing this now will give you better control over managing all your subsequent campaigns.

You will next need to establish your daily budget from the 10-day budget we discussed above. You need to commit enough to gather sufficient data to analyze your views, click-throughs, and sales adequately. This may cost you more money than it brings in initially, but as you gain experience, you will get more conversions, and your cost per click will decrease.

The next step is to select either the automatic or the manually targeted keywords, but you will select automatic for the first phase. Click Next Step, and complete the self-explanatory options to begin your custom ad campaign.

You can also select the option to begin now, but once you are redirected to your campaign dashboard, you can pause your campaign until you are ready to begin. Take advantage of this option as you prepare for your AP-Ads.

B. Discount Pricing

Sponsored Product Ads will bring more views of your Listing, and Discount Pricing will increase conversion rates (sales). So how do you discount prices, add to costs with large advertising costs and not go broke?

You discount your price from a higher price than you expected to get on an ongoing basis, and you budget your advertising costs within acceptable limits for a specified time during launch. How you go about managing the costs, discounts and specified times? Well, this is what an entrepreneur does.

Two types of customers will help you out during this phase of the launch. Some customers will equate price and quality, so by inflating the initial list price 10-15%, your product will be perceived as being "better." This perception will be bolstered by the improved product you created and terrific selling points included in your Listing.

Other customers love discounts and will be drawn by the thought of saving money. Perhaps these two customer types will be among your launch phase sales.

As you return to your normal price, you can still show this as some discount below your initial listed price, and this may have a positive impact on sales. There are many books and internet sources on the psychology of selling and pricing which may help in this area. (Search Amazon Books! Those books are out there.)

Amazon offers you the opportunity to **set up discount codes through Seller Central**. This allows you to limit the number of discounted sales that occur during the launch phase and to limit the number of purchases to only one per customer which is what you would like to do.

You can provide discounts from 5% to 80% which gives you the flexibility to control your discounts within a wide range to obtain reviews consistent with your strategy. Again, put this in your spreadsheet, so you know the impact on profits before you begin.

C. Product Reviews

Customers look at the number of product reviews and the number of stars associated with products as part of their purchasing decision. These are the stars shown on your product page.

As good as your Listing may be by now, you also need to appeal to the **customers who are looking for "social validation."** Social Validation is a powerful incentive for people to buy a product.

They will buy simply because others have bought. They will not buy if there are no reviews or only a few reviews. This is often an emotional response, not an intellectual, objective rationale.

For some customers, the emotional decision is made first, and then they seek intellectual affirmation of that decision. They may have connected with your images, or your Title, or some other appealing part of your Listing.

They will often read the 5-star reviews to see the details, to find out exactly why others thought this product was so good. They will then often adopt this as their reason to buy this product.

Customers also may make an intellectual decision to buy a product and will read both positive and negative reviews. They trust that the reviewers are telling them about quality, performance, and reliability in an unbiased way.

They will not buy a product with poor reviews, and a few reviews generally do not contain enough information about them to make the decision to buy a product. You will need reviews.

Not a good technique: You may find some advice from some outdated sources to use your friends and family to get some good reviews for your new Listing. This practice is not in accordance with the current Amazon terms and conditions.

There are several shortcuts like this that are banned, and you might think that Amazon will never find out. If they do find out, however, this tactic may not end well for you or your account.

1. Organic Product Reviews

So how do you get good product reviews? You ask your customers if they liked your product and to please give Amazon a review.

If they receive what you promised, and perhaps a little extra, your reviews will be good. By "a little extra," I mean higher quality than the competition, better packaging, good delivery times, sales literature on this and perhaps other products along with useful tips or instructions, and any small extras or replacement parts (if applicable).

Build this "extra" into your product design from the beginning. I discussed this earlier, but now you can see how this fits into your conversion rates through reviews.

To be more effective from the beginning of the "automatic" phase throughout the entire launch, you should also have a method of soliciting reviews while you advertise and your initial order is being sold during the launch phase.

You should send emails to every customer asking for their reviews automatically with an "autoresponder" software. Well "Yes," I do have a recommendation.

2. Solicit Reviews with Feedback Five

I am recommending Feedback Five because this **is the easiest autoresponder for new sellers on Amazon** to get up and running that I found after looking at many of them. If anyone finds an easier one, please let me know.

You do not need to learn a new program. No programming, just connect this to your account by following the directions.

Their wizard program connects automatically once you sign up and give the program the appropriate permissions to access your account. This program is free for the first block of sales; you can increase your cost in small increments as you grow your sales and need to send more emails.

You need sales to get product reviews, and you need reviews to get sales. I know this may seem like another chicken and the egg dilemma, but even a few reviews will make the ad campaign more effective.

Remember that reviews are not part of the A9 algorithm, but more good reviews will increase conversion rates, and this is a primary factor in A9. Think "flywheel" effect.

I still recommend the email solicitations, but customers are responding to these with an ever-decreasing frequency. I also see a significant increase in the number of customers who "opt out" of receiving emails, so never get them at all.

3. Product Reviews vs. Seller Feedback

There is some confusion among new sellers about product reviews and seller feedback; both are sometimes mistakenly referred to as reviews or feedback. We just discussed product reviews above and the "5-star" rating basis that appears on your product Listing page.

Feedback is also provided by your customers and likewise uses a "5-star" rating basis. This is the rating that appears next to your seller's name.

These two are further confused because you solicit product reviews and feedback regarding the buying experience with your email solicitations, and the customer often gets the two confused. They can give you poor feedback because they had a problem with your product, not with your service or shipment, but this then hurts your "performance" metrics with Amazon.

A poor rating can impact your ability to win the Buy Box, and your sales. Your seller's account can be suspended or canceled if you fail to meet Amazon's standards of performance.

I suggest that you go to your Performance tab routinely and follow up on any negative feedback. You might find that it is unjustified and get Amazon to remove it.

Feedback that is abusive or contains personal information will be removed. If you are FBA, then Amazon will take responsibility for the fulfillment experience, the review will remain, but it will appear as "strike-through" text and will not be counted against you.

As so often happens, the customer may discuss your product in that feedback post. **If your product is mentioned, Amazon will likely remove the feedback post** completely.

4. Price Discounts in Exchange for Reviews

Discounting your price to improve your SERP was covered separately as one way to increase sales, but there is also some evidence that **the deeper the discount, the more product reviews you will receive**. Using those Amazon discount coupons allows you to take advantage of this and control your costs to a fixed amount.

While this will increase the number of reviews per sale, calculate the cost of this strategy to see if you believe this is worthwhile. I would be hesitant to continue this beyond the initial launch phase.

Nevertheless, if your product is discounted appropriately during this launch phase, it follows that you should receive more reviews than you otherwise would get. I suggest that you look at the reviews received as you discount for improved sales before you get into deep discounting for additional reviews.

5. Solicit Reviews with "Stickers"

Some sellers are reporting successful campaigns to obtain product reviews by including some form of "stickers" on other forms of messages contained inside the product packages. Currently, one of the most successful is using a colorful sticker on their packages asking for reviews and giving directions to do this.

Others have used colorful notices, personal appeals in writing, and other similar methods. Many will work for a while, and then become less useful over time.

Check with Sellers Forum, and you will find others commenting on what has worked for them. Staying up to date with other sellers is an excellent way to keep your solicitations changing with the times, and they are generally good about sharing.

Be professional, and keep your comments brief and to the point. Someone will call you out if you are argumentative or show no understanding of the process, so read a great deal more often than you post, research before posting, and learn what is expected.

CHAPTER 10. POTENTIAL CONCERNS AND SOLUTIONS

There are excellent opportunities to expand your Amazon business by understanding how Amazon is designed to work with sellers like you. However, Amazon is not a benevolent organization. It is designed to make money for Amazon as well as the sellers, so be aware of how potential changes could negatively impact your business interests.

Consider what would happen if Amazon were to suddenly decide to offer a product like your private label product. Yes, after all that work and money.

Also, be aware of increased shipping costs, increased inventory costs, increased selling fees in the future, and tariffs on Chinese products. By being aware of these risks, you may be able to mitigate the impacts.

A. Products Sold by Amazon

Amazon has indicated that they intend to sell more products directly from "AMZ." This is consistent with their recent practice, so I see this announcement as acceleration to an existing program.

The data crunching software that Amazon already has in place is analyzing the millions of products being sold daily by third parties like you. The best-selling and the most profitable ones are known, and Amazon has the staff that reads those reports indicating the most profitable products for Amazon to source and sell directly.

A cynical person might suggest that these third-party sellers are being used to perform the market research for Amazon so they could increase their already substantial presence on their website. Amazon currently has a large staff that sources new products every day.

The billions of dollars available and knowledgeable staff will likely mean that Amazon will increase their bottom line by competing with already profitable items which they can source at a much lower cost than you or I can.

B. Make Your Product Less Vulnerable

While selecting your product niche and sourcing your private label, consider strategies for this possibility. I am going to advance a few ideas, and invite you to let me know of any others you might want to add:

- A product that has a unique design or other difficult to copy features might be a deterrent. The more different skill sets involved, the more likely this idea will drop to the bottom of their list.

- A product that you also sell on your website where you have a customer base are not exclusively from Amazon will help. Developing successful advertising skills so that you can expand this base using different channels and media will help insulate your sales from a challenger like Amazon. (See Multi-Channel Fulfillment in Chapter 11.)

- Creating a Branded Product on Amazon may also provide some protection, in part because of the additional programs available which mean additional revenue for Amazon. Not wanting to hurt these additional revenues and the legal protections of Trademarking would be important considerations.

- Just as selling only from a brick and mortar shop may not be the best long-term strategy today, selling exclusively on Amazon may also not be the best long-term strategy for tomorrow. You should consider beginning your sales experience, or expand your sales, with Amazon now, but with the concept of expanding into additional areas online following your initial successes.

C. Multiple Seller Accounts

I have recommended that most new sellers with limited experience consider having a partner, for several reasons. If you have your own account and want to add a partner for future activities, you will need a separate EIN (tax ID number), bank account and email address. You should also have a separate Amazon account.

Some have suggested that you have a second, "reserve" sellers account in case your primary account is suspended, for this or any other reason. I caution you that Amazon's terms and conditions do not normally permit that.

Like any other violation, unless you have extenuating circumstances acceptable to Amazon, this could end badly. Ask for permission consistent with the terms and conditions rather than seeking forgiveness.

You are expected to contact Amazon and receive permission which they will grant if you convince them that there is a good reason. In doing so, you will need to follow the Amazon terms and conditions.

One of Amazon's concerns is that these separate entities do not compete against each other by selling in the same category. I know that you would not do that, but Amazon may not be immediately convinced.

I would further suggest that you create a separate IP address for this second entity. The Amazon computers do track activities related to IP addresses.

One horror story concerns a visiting friend who sent a positive review of the friend's product to Amazon from the seller's home computer. Amazon computers flagged this activity and suspended the sellers account until many phone calls later when that was finally reversed.

One way, among many, to do that is to connect to the internet, not directly through your ISP (Internet Service Provider), but through a VPN (Virtual Private Network). All data from your device to the VPN will be encrypted, and you will be using an IP from the VPN rather than your ISP.

You will still need your ISP, but your VPN internet connections will have a different IP than when you connect directly through your ISP. I apologize for the geek-speak babble of letters, but the point is that the VPN will provide you with a separate IP address and Amazon will not get your two business entities confused.

D. Managing Negative Reviews

One of the dangers is that your seller's account may not meet the Amazon goal of minimizing negative Feedback. One negative review when you only have a few will impact your sales. Monitor this via the several metrics located in Seller Central Dashboard under "Performance" to see your company Feedback.

I have recommended Feedback Five to solicit favorable reviews or your products and your Feedback, but this is also a tool for you to monitor your reviews. You will receive a daily email telling you about the number of positive and negative product reviews you have, and you should take corrective action when negative reviews occur:

- Respond to negative reviews by clicking the "comment" feature located below each product review. Apologize and state your commitment to customer service.

  I would write this to impress other customers seeing this that you are someone who cares and want to make their experience a good one. This is not just intended for the negative reviewer.

- Contact the reviewer directly through buyer-seller messaging to make their problem disappear by writing a very polite response. Above all, do not in any way appear to be harassing them. Your goal is to have them remove the negative comment or update the review to make it better by your actions.

- Amazon will remove the review if you can convince them to do so. For example, when you are shipping FBA, and there is a problem with delivery or the shipment container, Amazon will take responsibility for that and remove any associated negative reviews.

  There are the occasional times when some reviews may violate Amazon's guidelines, and they will be removed accordingly. This is an easy one.

- Finally, I found that a negative review appeared for one of my products, but I did not sell to this customer. Amazon removed that once I had proven this to be the case.

E. Managing State Sales Taxes

I am not an accountant and will give you no tax advice. You should seek out an accountant who can answer your specific questions. I can only address this in a very general manner.

Amazon will collect state taxes on your behalf after you specifically set up this function with them. Call and chat with a representative if you decide to take advantage of this service.

Amazon will not pay those taxes for you. That will remain your responsibility.

Until recently, the major issue surrounding the state tax issue involves the **definition of "sales tax nexus" state by state**. You will likely have a sales tax nexus if you have more than a slight, cursory presence in a state.

Answering one of these questions in the affirmative likely means that you do:

- Are you located in the state?

- Do you have an office or employees in the state?

- Do your products reside at an FBA warehouse in the state?

It is complicated, and the only practical way I know to handle this is using TaxJar. This software can be tied to your seller's account and seems to be the accepted standard for compliance. Following their guidance may be the best advice if you are concerned.

You may need to file for state tax permits, and meet schedules for remitting taxes periodically. Once you file for a tax permit, the state will be expecting to hear from you on a regular basis. TaxJar can assist with all these requirements.

Most small sellers do not seem to be concerned, but they should be as sales increase substantially. Once you meet the "sales tax nexus" for Amazon in each state, your Shopify and other e-commerce sites also must be compliant.

Imagine getting an email from Amazon that a court order from the state of Massachusetts required them to report your inventory held in an Amazon warehouse last year. Many sellers did receive such an email in early 2018.

Certain Sellers holding inventory at an FBA warehouse within the state met the "nexus" statutes under state law that required their company to register, collect state sales tax, and pay those taxes according to Massachusetts regulations. The Massachusetts Department of Revenue wanted to compare the state sales receipts from these sellers to their records to see if state taxes were filed on time.

Amazon provides a list of tax advisors, software for calculating state taxes, and a tool for calculating where your inventory resides during the year. This letter from Massachusetts should not cause you indigestion if you have been complying with these state regulations throughout the year.

I present this Massachusetts tax story to you as a cautionary tale so that you can judge for yourself. Would this issue be a potential danger to your business if ignored?

The future requirements concerning small sellers collecting and paying state taxes were made less clear by a **recent U.S. Supreme Court ruling**. The ruling seems to suggest that more small sellers will be subject to this requirement, but everyone will have to follow developments as regulations are rewritten to incorporate this decision.

F. Tariffs on Chinese Products

I would not normally have thought that a section on tariffs would be relevant, but the current political climate suggests that this is a credible possibility. We have discussed the benefits for you to source your product from China, and much of this book is based on that premise.

Most of you are probably familiar with **the negative impacts of tariffs from Econ 101**. Tariffs generally are proposed initially as limited in scope, having some small benefit, and no significant risk of creating a trade war.

This has been true in some cases, but this is also how trade wars begin. If this country does have a trade war with China, your business may be at risk.

You can source from other countries; India is one possibility, but there are others. Finding new suppliers while competitors are trying to do the same and at the same time will be disruptive, even if you are successful over a reasonable time.

Trade wars also have a habit of expanding, often in unexpected ways so your new supplier may also eventually be at risk. You will need to find your way through this maze should it happen.

You should look at sourcing domestically, but domestic manufacturers will also be raising their prices. You might be better off in the long run by passing along the tariffs to the extent your customers are willing to pay them. Do not rush to change your suppliers.

There will be no winners if this occurs, so trying to prevent them may be the best way of coping. Speak to your congressperson.

G. Private Label Short Cuts

The basic premise behind creating your product that is better than your competitors' includes the assumption that the improvements you select belong to you or that you are free to use those improvements. You would not try to include a "better design" in your product that was a patented idea that belonged to someone else.

Use caution that you are not fooled by someone else who might try to do that. Micah is an experienced seller who found a beautifully designed product that a Chinese manufacturer was willing to sell him at a great price and allow him to use his logo on the product.

He purchased several thousand dollars of the product and successfully launched the product. Sales were increasing when Amazon blocked his sales because of an intellectual property complaint.

The manufacturer had used a name in describing his product that turned out to be a registered trademark by someone else. The manufacturer had ripped off a trademark product and sold it to Micah who then sold this as his own product.

Micah might have avoided this by using the online TESS (Trademark Electronic Search System) to search for registered trademarks as part of the USPTO.gov website. Note: TESS is also a good place to start when you are creating your trademark to see if it has already been taken (see Appendix E on Additional Resources).

Using this website will not catch all these potential traps, but it should be part of your due diligence when selecting potential products. I provided Micah's story because it illustrates one of many ways even an experienced seller can make mistakes when sourcing products.

The most secure approach is to use your own designs and follow the procedures outlined earlier. **Be wary of "shortcuts."**

H. Increased Selling Costs

Sales go up when you decrease your selling price and decrease when your price goes up. (Wow, who knew?) Amazon controls many of your costs, shipping to Amazon from your warehouse, shipping to your customer, the referral fees (cost of selling on Amazon), inventory fees, and other smaller fees associated with returns, etc.

You can try to reduce your cost of goods delivered, but you will likely need to increase your costs to cover these costs, and somewhat reduce your competitiveness as a result.

1. Shipping Costs to Customers

Amazon increased their charges for shipments from their warehouses to customers beginning February 22, 2018. They **changed the formula used to calculate the dimensional weight**; the calculation that makes shipping less dense packages more expensive.

The change will bring the Amazon formula in line with industry standards. The increases this year have not been typical, but they are significant. You will have no control over these or future increases, but these will reduce your profits unless you raise your prices.

Standard-size	Jan–Sept before February 2018	After February 2018	Percent Increase

Small Standard-Size (1 lb or less) Max: 15"x 12"x 0.75"	$2.41	$2.41	No increase
Large Standard-Size (1 lb or less) Max: 18"x 14"x 8"	$2.99	$3.19	**6.7% Increase**
Large Standard-Size (1 to 2 lbs) Max: 18"x 14"x 8"	$4.18	$4.71	**12.7% Increase**
Large Standard-Size (over 2 lbs, less 20 lbs) Max: 18"x 14"x 8"	$4.18 + $0.39/lb > 2 lbs	$4.71 + $0.38/lb > 2 lbs	**12.7% Increase,** but decreases slightly with increasing weight
Small Oversize Exceeds 20 lbs OR one of the max dimensions	$6.85 + $0.39/lb > 2 lbs	$8.13 + $0.38/lb > 2 lbs	**18.7% Increase,** but decreases slightly with increasing weight
Medium Oversize Exceeds 20 lbs OR one of the max dimensions	$9.20 + $0.39/lb > 2 lbs	$9.44 + $0.38/lb > 2 lbs	**2.6% Increase,** but decreases slightly with increasing weight

Some of these costs may be due to increased shipping costs to Amazon while some may just benefit their bottom line. I could only speculate about this, but these increases certainly will reduce your ROI and your bottom line.

Just be aware of future increases that may "squeeze" your profits and look at any potential alternatives. One of these alternatives could be the comparison with MFN (Merchant Fulfillment) to see how that compares with FBA.

Many factors outside this shipping cost increase would affect that decision, and hopefully, you are aware of those by now. However, I would expect your MFN shipping costs may also go up, and that might negate any temporary advantage.

2. Increased Shipping Costs to Amazon

By changing the dimensional weight calculation, your shipping costs will also increase the cost you pay for shipping product to Amazon from your warehouse. Remember that your investment is the cost to you for product delivered to Amazon warehouses and available for sale (including shipping and any preparation cost by Amazon).

You should look at this as an increase in your investment costs. Like increases in other costs, **this will negatively impact your bottom line**.

In addition to shipping costs, Amazon recently announced an increase in the storage cost of certain inventory. This increase was for larger items, but we should anticipate other inventory items may follow.

3. Litmus Paper Still Blue?

By this point, you have a good sense of the commitment required as well as the risks and the rewards of selling on Amazon. There will always more technical issues to be mastered; some included in this book and others that will arise as you begin to sell.

While there is more to learn from the last two chapters, you can check again to see if your litmus paper is still blue. I hope the best for you whatever your decision.

CHAPTER 11. EXPAND YOUR SUCCESS

N ow that you have your first successful product, you will need to find your second. One product does not a successful long-term business make. You will start this process over again, but at the same time, you should consider expanding your sales outlets and generating additional traffic.

A. Multi-Channel Selling

Multi-channel refers to using different platforms to sell your product. There are many online platforms available for selling your private label product.

Multi-channel sites that you should consider include eBay and your own (Shopify) webstore, but there are also many more that are more specific to a given product niche. For example, Etsy is ideal for arts and crafts, and other unique and personalized products.

A Google search of these services will also show you the many sales platforms that might provide targeted customers for your product niche. Also, note that this strategy will help protect your sales from compliance issues which may arise on the Amazon site (providing alternative sales platforms while resolving the Amazon compliance issues).

1. Multi-Channel Fulfillment Directly from Amazon

One method to begin the journey of selling on different platforms is by using your FBA Amazon account to fulfill sales generated on other websites.

This can dramatically increase your total sales and help with inventory control issues.

Discussions so far have concentrated on Amazon filling your orders through their FBA program, but they will also **fill the orders that you sell on other platforms**.

Amazon makes this easy by using Sellers Central to enter the buyer's information. Make a fulfillment request to Amazon, and you can use your Amazon account to ship your product from their warehouse:

- No need for you to fill your orders yourself.

- You do not need to maintain a separate inventory for those other platforms.

- You may find that Amazon shipping fees are less than your other options.

Amazon charges "fulfillment fees" for the shipping and handling, but does not charge a "referral fee" because the sale did not occur on the Amazon platform. You can select standard, expedited, or next day shipping options, and whether you want your product shipped in a plain box or one with the Amazon label.

See Amazon for current table of multi-channel shipping fees that would be charged to your account. Remember that you can use this approach for shipping Amazon inventory to any of the venues shown below.

2. Mechanics of Multi-Channel Fulfillment by Amazon

The mechanics of doing this begin in your Sellers Central account where you go to Settings and select Fulfillment by Amazon. One of the options on this page is Multi-Channel Fulfillment Settings; edit this by entering your product information.

To create an order for Amazon to ship, go to your inventory page in Sellers Central and select "Create Fulfillment Order." Complete the fields with the customer information, leaving the Order ID blank (it will be created automatically).

Fill in the quantity being shipped, and select Continue. This will take you to the shipping options where you can ship immediately, or select Hold if you are still waiting for payment.

You also have the option of including additional information to the customer in the Packing Slip field. Click Place Order when you are done.

3. Your Shopify Website

I do recommend that you consider your own website once you have your Amazon presence established. The Shopify.com option is a particularly attractive way to sell your product and is **geared for the beginning seller**.

The one caveat is that you will need to develop ways to drive traffic to your webstore. To do this, you will want to learn about advertising on Facebook and Google searches using SEO (Search Engine Optimization).

You will find other methods of enhancing the webstore's performance using autoresponders and incorporating the business model of the digital sales funnel discussed in Chapter 12. Another benefit of this approach: You own website should have **lower selling fees which will increase your ROI** on these sales.

There are paid services available (Google "multi-channel listing services") that can perform much of the integration of different sales platforms like eBay. You can list your product once and automatically have it appear on other platforms.

You can ship them directly from your facility, or you can use your existing FBA Amazon inventory and have Amazon ship them directly. You are concerned about ROI, but this is a very easy way to fill orders if you do not want to invest in a warehouse operation.

4. Advertising on Facebook

Advertising on Facebook should be an integrated effort to your Shopify site and expose traffic to your product. An insight into finding the target audience for those Facebook ads is a good place to begin.

A successful, cost-effective **campaign on Facebook requires a targeted audience** and not paying for ads to everyone. Otherwise, you pay for clicks that do not convert well and spend money with little return.

The Facebook audience Insights page will allow you to filter by location, age, gender, and interests among many other factors. You will want to test different audiences over time to improve your filters.

Begin your search with "Interests" and continue to narrow the results. Another filter would be the top 10 "Page Likes," and look for 70-80% plus related to your product, or product category.

Continue until you have 300,000 plus for that broader audience. Next divide the broader audience further into three segments based on similarities in relevant subscriptions, relevant personalities/influencers, or relevant websites/pages.

You will be able to refine this list based on your product so that you can design an ad for each segment. Set a small daily budget to $5 per ad set.

This should show results quickly, over a few days, and you can better optimize these subsets while selecting the best one for a larger campaign. My larger point is not to make you an expert in Facebook advertising, but to give you a sense of what is involved so that you can pursue this further.

You will want to utilize the Facebook pixel which you can install when visitors reach your landing page (or Shopify store) to leave their email address and pick up their promotional coupon. This pixel is a code that attaches to a visitor and allows you to collect data as the visitor leaves your site.

This is a way to continue to reach those who showed interest but did not provide their emails. You can extend this outreach for up to a year.

Note: you cannot install a pixel if they are taken directly to your Amazon listing. You can create your landing page for visitor click-throughs or use a service like AMAZON Promoter or ClickFunnels.

B. Take Your Product Global

Amazon makes it relatively easy to sell your product in other countries. You can readily sell in Canada and Mexico, and you can do this from one account, the Unified North American Account.

You can also sell in Great Briton and the **Pan European markets** of Germany, France, Italy and Spain using Amazon's European Unified Account. Keep in mind that just because your product was successful in the USA, that does not guarantee success in another country.

The same processes you learned earlier to get your product to this stage, can be replicated in other countries. Amazon makes it very easy to use your sellers account to do this.

To see how this might be done and some of the nuances involved, find the YT series by Jungle Scout on the **Million Dollar Case Study Europe**. Greg Mercer has an excellent, detailed series on how to use the Jungle Scout system to find and source products unique to those specific markets, all the way through Listing and Importing.

C. Talking to Amazon

You can talk to Amazon, or chat if you prefer, about any issue where you need help. I have found them to be **very helpful and conscientious**, perhaps in part because you are asked to grade their performance after each contact.

You will find contact information through Seller Central. But "talking" is just one method and one I use for my specific product issues. They have been very prompt when I ask them to call me, or you can also "chat" immediately with a representative.

Make liberal use of the sellers' forum where you can search and find threads related to specific issues that others wanted to be discussed. Most common issues have been discussed and generally resolved by an Amazon staff member within these threads.

Not only will you find answers to your general question, but you will also often find related threads that discuss peripheral questions that will be useful. I suggest that you write down some issues that have come to mind during your reading and spend time on the forum becoming familiar with this valuable tool.

D. Repeat Your Success

Repeat and improve upon your success. Now that you have your first private label, you will want to do this again with the idea of establishing a process that you can repeat, and one that gets better with each iteration.

You used a process, not exactly as I described it because my suggestions were only guidelines, but you found a formula that worked for you. Review what you did and note those variables that were most important.

Did you use the Amazeowl platform shown in Chapter 5, only a part of it, or combined it with Jungle Scout? Take the time to draft an outline of your procedure and what you found to be the most important parts.

You may have taken shortcuts with some sections of the book; perhaps you did not analyze your competition as well as you could have, or perhaps one of your product launch exercises wasted money because of your inexperience. Write down your process to improve on your work.

Before you memorialize your process and it becomes just OK, make it the best it can be, and then repeat your successful process. Successful businesses review and improve their process after each new product.

I guess that many new sellers will not adequately explore increasing sales through driving traffic from outside Amazon. Go back through the discussions on using Google SEO (Search Engine Optimization) backlinks, and then do more research on other successful techniques using Google.

Do the same for YT (YouTube) and using techniques employed by Amazon Affiliates. Techniques used by ClickFunnels and other online digital marketing efforts can be immensely rewarding.

I was impressed by the ingenuity and number of different techniques available. Make it your mission to explore and implement just one of these outside traffic options every quarter (or periodically).

Improve your process based on experience and a changing environment, and it will serve you well. You must reinvest your profits, improve your skills, learn new techniques for improving sales (the life-blood of any business), and increase your product offerings to be successful in the long run.

I am confident that you will succeed with a positive, adaptive attitude using this book as a foundation for future experiential study. I was encouraged to see that your litmus test was still blue.

CHAPTER 12. OUTSIDE TRAFFIC

For your first product, I believe that the SP-Ads will be all that most new products will need to start the "flywheel effect." (That was discussed at the beginning of Chapter 9.) However, there are also techniques that can be used to continue to drive new traffic to your listing; traffic originating from outside the Amazon platform.

A. Integrate Online Presence and Amazon

The reasons to expand your online presence to platforms beyond Amazon were discussed in the previous chapter. I assume that you will eventually do this, and from your (Shopify) website, you can drive additional launch traffic directly to your new product page.

As part of your Shopify experience, you will likely have a Facebook ad presence and have developed skill sets at driving traffic to that website. These same skill sets can be used during your launch phase to drive sales in the future.

You will likely enjoy an improved ROI from sales made on your (Shopify) website because you eliminate Amazon sales costs. You do not want to cannibalize these sales, but you can divert some sales to your Amazon product page during the launch phase.

One technique is to promote the 2-day delivery for Prime customers. Another is to use sales codes on your Shopify or (another e-commerce site) that you can get for your Amazon page.

You can find these coupon codes from your Seller Central account where you can control the number and the discount for each code. (Remember from the product launch discussion?)

B.   Digital Sales Funnel

There are other online skill sets that you will develop as you follow my advice to diversify that can be directed at enhancing your launch strategy. One method derives from a digital marketing approach called a sales funnel that could be used effectively.

That approach would take a separate book to discuss, but there are many online sources (see YT on sales funnel marketing) where you can get an overview of the skill sets involved in driving traffic. You will find that just the "driving traffic" portion is a complex subject with many derivations in sources and techniques.

You do not need to be an expert in this, just select one and find out how it works for you. Limit your cost and only try this after you see the financial impact on your spreadsheet.

Succinctly, you drive paid traffic to a website called a "landing page" where you advertise your product, without any of the Amazon restrictions you have on your product page. You can then send this traffic directly to your Amazon page for the purchase.

You can also solicit their email addresses to build a list of future purchasers, and make this attractive by offering them a discount coupon for use on your Amazon product page. This list can be used later to send them to your other e-commerce sites where your ROI should be better.

This is likely a new concept for you, and I suggest that you might look at some sites that make this easier for the novice, like AMZPromoter. A few minutes on this site will give you a simple overview of the process, but do not get the idea that the process does not require effort.

The practice is very doable, but it is another skill set that requires time and effort to learn your craft. I mention this because you may want to spend the effort doing this later, but this is not part of launching your first product.

C.   Amazon Affiliate Program

Amazon has a large Affiliate program that can and should be employed to drive traffic. Officially this is called The Amazon Associates Program.

One signs up on Amazon and is issued the right to use codes placed within URL links that direct customers to your product page. The Affiliate is incentivized to promote your page because she receives a commission for every sale.

Often, the Affiliate creates a website (called a "landing page" which was discussed earlier) to advertise your product. Sometimes a direct ad is used to bring traffic to this landing page, or the affiliate can use an email list to generate traffic predisposed to purchase your product.

You can provide support, such as videos, for these Affiliates to encourage and make their efforts more productive as they work on your behalf. The Affiliate usually posts these on their landing pages to help sell your product before directing traffic to your product page, but they can also be used in direct ads to send traffic directly through their affiliate link.

There are several venues for displaying these Affiliate links including posting them on appropriate blogs and even within the description section of YTs related to your product. Affiliates only need to find an appropriate YT video, or blog, with followers likely interested in your product.

The Affiliate sends an email to the producer and asks that they include the affiliate link in their YT description or blog for a modest fee. If the fee is modest and the traffic substantial, everyone wins.

These support videos are a good way to get videos and other enhanced content materials in front of customers that you will not be allowed to do on your product page until you are Branded and have Enhanced Content permission. The reason that you want to have Enhanced Content on your product page eventually is that it works, it sells.

Using the Affiliate approach is a shortcut to utilizing these sales tools. This is a good approach and a potential win-win.

Do not exclude providing videos because this is not a skill set you have. Your virtual assistant will produce a video to your specifications for very little money.

You may want to become an affiliate yourself in the future. You can send traffic to your site and pick up an additional fee, up to 10% depending on the product's category.

For example, if you were in the home improvement, lawn & garden, or pet products categories, you could earn an additional 8% if someone used your link and purchased your product. If you follow the rule of thumb, one-third purchase cost, one-third Amazon and other fees, and one-third profit, what additional ROI would you make for that referral?

Do the math, and you will find that is equivalent to an additional 24% ROI on that one sale. (ROI of 33% and now that is 41% or approximately 8/33 = 24% more.)

D. SEO (Google) Traffic

SEO (Search Engine Optimization) is the practices designed to increase your Page Ranking results when someone searches for your product on Google. The specific Google algorithm for Page Ranking is different than the one used by Amazon, but they try to accomplish the same end.

When someone searches for "coffee mugs," each search engine wants to provide the most "relevant page" links possible so that the searcher is not disappointed, but instead finds exactly what they wanted. One of the major factors for this algorithm involves "backlinks"; these are links (a URL) to your product page that appear on the websites of others.

These backlinks are often shown as blue and contain a word related to your product. The websites containing your backlinks should be credible and related to your product to make your page relevant.

For example, if you were selling coffee mugs, then you would want your backlink on a highly regarded site about the world's best coffees, not on a blog about building log houses. I know that you could draw a straight line between your coffee mugs and log houses, but the algorithm cannot.

Some of these backlinks will be coded (in their URL codes) as "dofollow" and others as "rel=donotfollow." Only the "dofollow" backlinks help in your Page Ranking.

My point is that there are significant technical issues that most of us are not interested in learning, but we may like the idea of getting traffic from the use of SEO results. Use an online assistant to do this.

Provide your assistant with your product name, product category, KWs (Key Words) that you want SEO to associate with your product and your product page URL. Provide them with the product information that they need to create the backlinks and place them.

Do the research yourself on the most credible sites to place your backlinks. Why? Because you are the one who knows what a relevant blog or other site is, and you may find other uses for these sites later.

This is valuable information that you may be able to use for other promotions later even if you are unable to get your backlink on that site now. You will follow up on the results, and likely commission other assistant "gigs" to do the same to make this technique even more effective.

Note: I have mentioned Fiverr and Upwork in the past, but become familiar with each so that you have the experience to find the appropriate virtual assistant when the need arises. The online landscape is constantly changing, and a Google search will provide other sites dealing with specific skills.

E.   YT (YouTube) Traffic

You will not be able to use videos initially on Amazon, but they are excellent sales tools. Use YT (YouTube) instead to create a 5-minute product review to showcase all the great features of your product.

Write the review, or even better make a video and use this as a model for your virtual assistant to turn into a polished product. You will be amazed at the quality of video possible for such a low cost.

To bring YT traffic, you need to do the following:

- You will want to change the name of your YT file to your targeted KWs.

- Your Title should be similar in concept to your Amazon Title in that you want to showcase your KWs in an easily read format.

- Your Description is also like the Amazon Description that includes a detailed review of the benefits of your product for the customer (what problem it solves for them), but also to explain what the video does, why they should watch it.

- Change the Properties TAG of your video by right clicking on your video, clicking details, and adding your KWs.

- Go to advance setting and change the Category as appropriate for your video.

- Click "publish."

To bring Google traffic to your video, you need to go through the same steps shown above for SEO (Google) Traffic. The major difference is that you will use the URL of your YT video rather than your product page URL.

Like similar issues where you do not want to develop this expertise yourself, use a virtual assistant. My suggestion is that you outsource everything like this that could reduce the time you have to concentrate on your business.

CHAPTER 13. KNOW YOUR NICHE AND COMPETITORS

I magine that you could find data on the demand level of your niche, seasonal demand changes, KW searches, price levels and the impact of reviews. You will also be able to find detailed information about individual competitors.

You will see changes they made (with detailed annotations), and the impacts on their operations. These data will give you a tremendous advantage over competitors who do not invest the time and learn how to investigate their Niche and competitors.

Begin the analysis by first going to the Amazeowl Competitors and Reports Tabs where you will first identify competitors. Look at the individual sellers (select them one by one) that appear and delete those that you do not consider your competitors.

This may be because of their products, prices, quality, or other disqualifying factors. For those remaining competitors, you will be able to get an insight into many of their business metrics. This will also define your Niche for analysis purposes.

Beyond Amazeowl used in the first two sections, you will find resources to locate additional data and analysis tools. Those additional sections in Amazeowl require more effort, but this is part of learning your craft and will separate you from the less successful.

BEGINNERS' GUIDE (STEP BY STEP) TO SELLING PRIVATE LABEL PRODUCTS ON AMAZON FBA

A. Analyze Your Product Niche with Amazeowl

I am going to show you how to do all that and more with the free version of Amazeowl. Collecting these data can be done without extensive, time-consuming research.

Review the data below and record those which you believe are important to your decision. Some are "raw" data for you to evaluate, but others have been analyzed for you by the software and presented in a format that ranks results in a "star" format (like Amazon reviews).

Like all the other data you collected, add these to your spreadsheet for objective review later when you can create a plan to exploit this knowledge. I continue to use the term "your spreadsheet," but some data, like those below (any many others in previous chapters), should be in a separate spreadsheet.

1. Demand and Ease of Entry: Both are "star" values indicating two critical factors where the analysis has been done for you. You would like both criteria to approach "5-stars" so that the total approaches "10". My sense is that 6 to 8 would be acceptable.

   Note also that you may have competitors in this analysis that you would not consider your true competitors after a more in-depth analysis of the market. I view this as a very rough indicator.

   However, make sure that the first step in this process is to show only your best-guess of true competitors. See the "Competitors and Reports" screen where you eliminate those you judge as not actually in your niche.

2. Keyword Monitoring tab Search Volume (# searches per month on Amazon), Ease of Entry ("stars" format based on # reviews), number of Competitors, Median Price, Total number of Reviews. (Note: this section of Amazeowl uses Merchant Words to collect much of the data shown, and if you do not have a subscription ($60/mo) you will be limited in the number of Keyword searches conducted each day. This is not a serious limitation to learning the concepts and finding data on keyword searches in the beginning but can be if you get serious about this step.

3. Research tab: Monthly Searches will give you a Google Trends graph of the number of searches to get a sense of whether the generic product is trending up over time. You will also be able to see the impact of seasonality on sales of your product.

   a. Demand Level (place your cursor over this location) will give you a sense of the demand base on the # of sellers and the # of searches.

   b. Competitors will show the # of competitors and the median # of reviews.

   c. Ease of Entry Level (place your cursor over this location) will give you a sense of the barrier caused by # of reviews and the listing quality of competitors.

B. Evaluating Competitors using Amazeowl

Amazeowl provides important information on competitors through the Competitors and Reports Tabs. You will gain insight into the business metrics of individual competitors in the tabs below.

1. Stats tab: Find graphs on sales and short-term price history of all competitors. There is a large amount of information to understand in the aggregate by viewing these colorful graphs. Just get a sense of these graphs (trending up/down, volatile, "stand-out performers") and then look at the graphs of individual competitors one at a time (by color).

2. Competitors tab: Select the Title of a specific competitor to see:

   a. History tab: is one the most interesting because it shows details about what changes were made over time and the impact that change had on BSR (Best Seller Rankings). Many changes indicate a very active and committed seller (tough competitor), and you should also get a sense of the importance of certain changes on your listing.

    b.   Price history: Remember that price stability is one reason you are creating your private label. This is an opportunity to assess that.

    c.   Number of reviews: Get a sense of how long it might take you to get reviews if you follow that competitor's example.

3. Keyword tab: The colorful keywords in varying sizes indicate the relevance of those words to your competitors. Note that you can view these by Titles, Bullets or Descriptions. Make a note of the words most prominent in the title for subsequent review.

4. Keywords Ranking tab: Will show you how well your competitors are ranking for a specific generic keyword.

C. Quantify the Listings of Competitors

By analyzing KWs of competitors, you can both rate them, see their weaknesses and strengths, and improve your Listing. Download free software called The Hoth.

Start by inserting what you consider keywords from the dominant seller's Listing into KW software. There is no need to also look at the bullets and description for now.

The Hoth shows you the number of searches conducted on Google with this, and derivations of this keyword. By considering these results, you will be better able to select keywords for the other competitor Listings for analysis.

Note the "real winners" so that you can consider these for your Listing. This process will take some time, but it will yield a wealth of keyword information that can make your Listing the "best in class."

Augment this process by taking some of these keywords and begin typing them into the Amazon search bar. Amazon will try to complete your typing with suggestions. These are keywords used by customers seeking your product or similar products.

Add the relevant keyword searches to your database of keywords from The Hoth. Try to identify the principal generic keywords most often used by potential customers.

Google Adwords is another free source of finding keywords, and I recommend that you add this method to the two above. Merchant Words is one of the better programs for keyword searches.

I have not included them only because of their relative cost compared to these two free methods. As you search Google for similar services, you will find several free services.

1.   Rate Competitors Titles, Photos, Bullets, and Descriptions

Jungle Scout has a free service which allows you to paste the ASIN codes of competitors and get a quick overview of their Listing. Use it, but this is just one data point, and you need more specific information like that suggested above to understand this rating better.

While some of the tools suggested in this chapter rate Listings on the number of words used in Listings, and the number of photos provided, your judgment on the title, photos, bullets, and descriptions should also be done qualitatively. Are the bullets and description adequate to convey the features? More importantly, do they describe a solution for the customers' needs?

Customers search to satisfy a need, and your product Listing should clearly show how that need is met. Make a list of how these needs are satisfied from the customer's perspective and bullet point them. Use the description to describe further and complete these points. Rate how well each of your competitors understands this concept.

Photos are the principal tool you have available to sell your product. Everyone will see your main photo, and they will not look further if this is done poorly.

As discussed earlier, pictures should be professionally done. I would suggest a minimum of 1500 by 1500 pixels on a white background.

They do not have to be expensive; outsource them online, but do not do them with your cell phones and expect the best outcome. Perhaps a competitor has only provided a few, not the full seven allowed, and this will be to your advantage.

Titles contain the keywords that will be used by Amazon in searches. Bullets, description and the back-end listing line that specifically asks for keywords, are well down the priority list for the A9 algorithm that looks for keywords.

Here is the trade-off, do you "pack keywords" into the title or do you describe your product in more human terms to your customers? You will not be found if those keywords are not there.

As you know from previous discussions, the correct answer is a hybrid, but with emphasis on using "human terms." However, many competitors will pack keywords, not tell the customer their story, only state what their product is and not what it does or how it satisfies their needs.

You have several qualitative factors to review in this subsection, but make enough notes on each that you can justify an overall rating for their Listings. If you rate a Listing as "poor," you will have a much easier time overtaking that competitor.

2.   Sponsored ads and Online Presence

When you search on Amazon, you will see products shown as "Amazon Sponsored Products." The seller paid to have their products appear in a prominent location when you used those keywords.

This was discussed more in the section on product launches, but for now, just note which competitors are using this form of advertising. These are the competitors who will generally be in your class, knowledgeable sellers who are actively managing their sales.

Conduct a Google search for competitors to see where else they might be selling their product. They may have a Shopify store, eBay sales or other proprietary online presence. This will give you a better idea of how well established their product may be.

I use a free product (Chrome extension) called Zally that magically appears when I go to a Listing. There is a lot of information available from this "black box of a pop-up," including a listing of all the sellers and their inventories.

When I see a seller with both an FBA and an MFN designation, I suspect that this product may also be listed on eBay, or elsewhere. This is another indication that this seller may be a tough competitor.

The reason for evaluating sponsored ads and online presence is because you need to understand the nature of your competition. When you find a niche that has many strong competitors, understand that your job has become more difficult. Include this information in your spreadsheet so that you select the product niche best for attaining your goals.

3. Evaluate Competitors' Packaging

In your first Amazeowl "Hunt for Products," you limited your search as to size and weight to minimize shipping and handling costs. I recall finding a potential product based on different criteria, without regard to size. I was looking for a product weighing less than 5 pounds, but with other attractive characteristics.

One of the results was a rolled-up bathroom mat, longer than 18 inches. The mat could be folded and repackaged into a box that did meet the 18-inch limit which significantly decreased the FBA Fulfillment Fees, increasing my profit. Of the potential competitors with similar products, only one had done this, and I redesigned my packaging and benefited from his work.

Once you have completed the search for products meeting your ideal characteristics, you might want to expand your thinking to other areas where most people do not often search. Realize that you are compromising your shipping and handling costs, potentially taking air shipment away as an option as you increase the size and weight restrictions.

I am not recommending this be done now. Just remember that this is an option for later.

4. Parting Words

You now have the basics of selling your PL product. There are areas that I could only touch upon, but further research along with mastering the skills discussed should lead you closer to reaching your goals. Your success will depend upon the commitment you make.

My goal was to provide you with a knowledge needed for you to make the decision to begin or not. If your litmus paper is still blue, I wish you a profitable journey. If not, I hope that this book has saved you from financial losses and time you can better use to enjoy life.

APPENDIX A. SOFTWARE RESOURCES

T his is a collection of software and resources you will want to become familiar with when you become serious about selling on Amazon. Most of this is free, or low cost. Note that when this book was published, some of the recommended software was not functioning at full capacity because of an industry-wide technical issue. I assume this is temporary, and functionality will have been restored by the time you read this book.

A. Chrome Extensions

The following software products are free, easy to install and run from your Chrome Browser. To install the Chrome Extensions listed below, use your Chrome Browser and go to Google Store Chrome Extension: Search for the specific extension (see below) in the "Search Extensions" box https://chrome.google.com/webstore/category/extensions

- Click on the blue "+ Add To Chrome" button to add one of these extensions
- Note: "YT" stands for YouTube, and provides additional information for those add-ons.
-
1. **Keepa**: Shows the cost history of a product on Amazon, and the number of sellers over time (3 months or a year). **Keepa YT**: https://www.youtube.com/watch?v=QSnloPazwU8

2. **CamelCamelCamel.com** Is the web site by this is also a Chrome extension, "camelizer" basically shows the price of a product over time; not materially

different   from   Keepa.   **YT**   **on**   **using**   **both:**
https://www.youtube.com/watch?v=qBjZNjLxpEU

3. **HowMany? (#?):** Free version can be used 5 times a day to show the number of items in inventory. (consider Zally instead)

4. **FBA Calculator:** Shows the Amazon costs associated with a specific listing, and often gives the estimated sales/month (consider Zally instead).

5. **Unicorn Smasher**: Similar to AMZScout and Jungle Scout; works on "search results" page rather than the one page for a specific product, and shows results for all items on that page.

6. **AMZScout**: Free (short time) trial period, but $49 for extended use: Similar to Jungle Scout ("JS" costs $110-$200). AMZScout offers more than the inexpensive version of JS (Listing Quality, Min Price, # of Sellers, Weight): (consider Zally instead).

7. **AMZpecty**: (not free) Amazon Seller Tool to check competitor available stock/quantity on-demand via Chrome Extension or Daily Product Snapshot via Web Application!

B. Non-Chrome Extensions

Below are not Chrome Extensions, but are valuable sources of data when you are evaluating products.

8. **Google Trends:** Will show a "normalized" or relative level of interest over time for a prospective keyword phrase. It also allows you to compare the level of interest among potential target phrases.

9. **Zally similar to JS, AMZscout, FBA Calc**

10. **Calculator and How Many#**
    - It takes just 1-second to enter your buy price and discover your profit, ROI, margins, stock levels, sales per month & much more...
    - Know your competitors' current stock level AND the total volume in the marketplace AND the average per seller!

- Save Your Findings: Save, share, export, and review all your findings! Easy!

C. Keyword Assistance

Keyword Assistance: for use when creating your Listing and evaluating listings of your competitors.

11. **Keyword Everywhere:** Get monthly search volume, cost per click and competition data for your list of keywords. You can copy keywords directly from Excel and download them as an Excel, CSV or PDF file. Select any set of words on any website and right click to get the keyword data for the selected words

    You can view keyword search volume, cost per click and competition data, on many websites like Google Analytics, Google Webmaster Tools (now called Search Console).

12. **Scientific Seller Keyword** The World's Slowest Keyword Tool (And How it Steadily Wins the Race) http://app.scientificseller.com/keywordtool#/

13. Other keyword assistance: **Ubersuggest** https://ubersuggest.io/

14. **Amazon keyword Suggestions Scraper**: Help you to find keywords that people are typing into the Amazon search box.

D. Finding Products Software

Miscellaneous sources of data when looking for products to sell.

15. Note: some of these URL site names have been shortened using **goo.gl URL Shortener (Unofficial)** where you can shorten long URLs into much shorter versions. I suggest you try this site just to become familiar with the

concept. It is often used because traditional URLs can become large and look "intimidating" to the user.

16. **Jungle Scout** has free software at their site: https://www.junglescout.com/amazon-product-research-resources/
    - SALES ESTIMATOR Instantly see an estimate of monthly sales for any Amazon product by category.
    - THE LISTING GRADER Use this free tool to evaluate how optimized your Amazon listing is, and how it can be improved.

17. **Amazeowl** is free (more features available for a fee) software; it is used as a tool to find which products you may want to sell. Watch the YouTube video (57 minutes) and see if this interest you. https://www.youtube.com/watch?v=5X333sK4SAE

    Note: Compare the free Amazeowl App with this Jungle Scout Web App ($40/mo) video to see two methods (with similar criteria) for finding products (57 minutes). https://www.youtube.com/watch?v=_8DOnWmHHwQ

APPENDIX B. AMAZON UNIVERSITY

Amazon uses this term in a more restrictive manner, but I mean this as an all-encompassing term to suggest that sellers can find the resources needed to understand how to use the Amazon platform on Sellers Central. Once you have opened your account and began to explore Sellers Central, you will find videos, PDF files, a sellers' forum, and constantly evolving and improving sources. Also, you will have the support staff available through Sellers Central available for an instant chat or by telephone.

A. One of these is a guide to the overall process of listing products by sending them into an Amazon warehouse. I am presenting this to give you a sense of the resources you will find.

Guide to basic mechanics: https://images-na.ssl-images-amazon.com/images/G/01/fba-help/QRG/FBA-Quick-Start-Guide.pdf

B. You will find helpful advice such as that below. Note that some of the jargon will become easier to understand as you proceed through the materials and begin sending the product to Amazon. What is a commingled inventory option?

1. Inspect your product to ensure that it has a physical barcode (UPC, EAN, ISBN, JAN, GTIN, etc.).

2. If the product does have a physical barcode, check your listing to verify that the physical UPC/EAN/ISBN/JAN number corresponds to the ASIN that you plan to send to Amazon. If the physical barcode number does not correspond to the ASIN listing, contact Seller Support for assistance.

3. If no physical barcode is present, you must label the product. You can print Amazon product labels from the Label Products step in the shipment creation workflow (see page 10).

C. Amazon recommends having the following materials on hand:
- Product and shipment prep workstation
- Thermal or laser printer
- Scale for weighing boxes
- Measuring tape to measure boxes
- Printed copies of How to Prep Products, How to Label Products, Shipment Requirements: Small Parcel, and Shipment Requirements: LTL & FTL (found at the end of this guide)
- Product labels (printed from your account, if applicable
- Tape
- Dunnage (packing materials)
- Boxes
- Polybags (at least 1.5 mils thick)
- Opaque bags (adult products only)
- Bubble wrap
- "Sold as Set" or "Ready to Ship" labels (if applicable)

Need packaging and prep materials? Check out the Amazon Preferred Product Prep and Shipping Supplies Store to learn more about how Amazon can help with your shipping supply needs.

D. Assign inventory to FBA. The following is the type of detailed instructions provided. Reading this while in front of your Sellers Central account makes the effort intuitive after the first couple of iterations.

1. Once you're ready to create your first shipment, the next step is to assign your inventory to FBA. Log in to your Seller Central account and go to Inventory > Manage Inventory.

2. Select products you would like to include as FBA listings by checking the box next to them in the far-left column.

3. From the Actions pull-down menu, select Change to Fulfilled by Amazon.

4. On the next page, click the Convert & Send Inventory button.

5. Once you've converted your listings, follow the instructions in the shipment creation workflow to create your first shipment to FBA.

Note: If you are not ready to create your first shipment after converting inventory to FBA, click the Convert button to convert your listing without creating a shipment. When you're ready, you can start your shipment by following the instructions in the Create an FBA shipment from converted inventory section.

Listing review: If we notice a potential issue with one or more of your listings, we may notify you before you send your inventory to Amazon and provide instructions for making needed adjustments. Potential issues might require that you enter additional information, such as package dimensions, or relist your product to align with the correct ASIN.

E. Example of posting from the Sellers Forum and one of several replies.

Original post: I am creating a brand new product, creating a new listing as well. Do I need to purchase UPC Labels from GS1 website (Hella Expensive!) or am I fine with just the FNSKU number that Amazon generates for your from your Seller Account? Please help!

Reply: You will need a UPC to list your items on Amazon unless you are a registered brand on Amazon. For FBA, the FNSKU labels are what you will need to use.

You can buy some UPCs on the bay if you need them. Leading Edge Bar Codes sells legit GS1 registered barcodes in lots. Many sellers have used them and have had no issues.

APPENDIX C. AFFILIATE FEE SCHEDULE

As an Amazon Affiliate, you can earn additional fees by driving traffic directly to your product page. Amazon provides the following incentives for you to do that by Product Category.

Product Category	Fixed Standard Program Fee Rates
Amazon Gift Cards, Wine	0.00%
Video Games & Video Game Consoles	1.00%
Televisions, Digital Video Games	2.00%
PC, PC Components, DVD & Blu-Ray	2.50%
Toys	3.00%
Amazon Fire Tablet Devices, Dash Buttons, Amazon Kindle Devices	4.00%
Physical Books, Health & Personal Care, Sports, Kitchen, Automotive, Baby Products	4.50%

Digital Music, Grocery, Physical Music, Handmade, Digital Videos	5.00%
Outdoors, Tools	5.50%
Headphones, Beauty, Musical Instruments, Business & Industrial Supplies	6.00%
Apparel, Amazon Element Smart TV (with Fire TV), Amazon Fire TV Devices, Jewelry, Luggage, Shoes, Handbags & Accessories, Watches, Amazon Echo Devices	7.00%
Furniture, Home, Home Improvement, Lawn & Garden, Pets Products, Pantry	8.00%
Amazon Fashion Women, Men & Kids Private Label, Luxury Beauty, Amazon Coins	10.00%
All Other Categories	4.00%

APPENDIX D. ADDITIONAL RESOURCES

Jungle Scout has several series of videos showing the complete process of selling products on Amazon from A to Z by Mr. Greg Mercer. The first one is the Million Dollar Project, and the others build upon this series on YT. I strongly recommend that you consider spending the 20 plus hours watching each one to learn better one approach which has proven successful. The following link will get you started, or just search for Greg Mercer and Jungle Scout, or Million Dollar Project.

https://www.youtube.com/playlist?list=PLblj9-Let4em0_bbdD8qTk3DrwhnTf41Q.

1. **Amazeowl** has several training videos that show you a great deal of detail information (useful, need-to-know) about the product sourcing process by Mr. Seth Kniep. This YT site should get you started, or just search Amazeowl and Seth Kniep and you will find many training videos on how to use their product. These are exceptionally well-done training videos.

https://www.youtube.com/watch?v=5X333sK4SAE

2. **Mr. Skip McGrath** has an excellent newsletter that will keep you up to date on what is happening on Amazon and other platforms. The subscription to his newsletter if free and worth your time. He has information from guest writers as well as his articles that contain current information that is difficult to gather from other sites. Just google Skip McGrath newsletter.

http://www.skipmcgrath.com/newsletters/

3. **SellerLabs** has timely articles on selling on Amazon intended to keep you up to date on what has happened and what is anticipated. They also present tutorials on topics needed to be a successful seller on Amazon. The

subscription is free so check it out to see if you find it worth your time as I did.
https://www.sellerlabs.com/

4. **Anthony Bui-Tran:** **Seller Tradecraft** is another source of best selling techniques and how to organize your business. You will likely be using Fiver for your first product, and VAs (Virtual Assistants) later to help grow your business beyond your initial product. I am including a YT from Mr. Bui-Tran on hiring VAs, but this is another source of continuing help which you will want to follow.
https://www.youtube.com/watch?v=0YZWuyWpB3A

5. Mica, lost some money because he failed to perform his due diligence with a new supplier, but perhaps this incident will help someone else avoid a similar fate. You will also want to use this site to search your potential trademarks.
https://www.uspto.gov/trademarks-application-process/search-trademark-database

The **Trademark Electronic Search System (TESS)**. This search engine allows you to search the USPTO's database of registered trademarks and prior pending applications to find marks previously registered.

APPENDIX E. SHIPPING COST TO CUSTOMERS (TABLE)

A mazon increased their charges for shipments from their warehouses to customers in February 2018. These are the "pick, pack and ship" charges paid by the seller.

Standard-size	Shipping Costs to Customer
Small Standard–Size (1 lb or less) Max: 15"x 12"x 0.75"	$2.41
Large Standard–Size (1 lb or less) Max: 18"x 14"x 8"	$3.19
Large Standard–Size (1 to 2 lbs) Max: 18"x 14"x 8"	$4.71
Large Standard-Size (over 2 lbs, less 20 lbs) Max: 18"x 14"x 8"	$4.71 + $0.38/lb > 2 lbs
Small Oversize Exceeds 20 lbs OR one of the max dimensions	$8.13 + $0.38/lb > 2 lbs
Medium Oversize Exceeds 20 lbs OR one of the max dimensions	$9.44 + $0.38/lb > 2 lbs
Large Oversize Exceeds 20 lbs OR one of the max dimensions	$73.18 + $0.79/lb > 2 lbs

Made in the USA
San Bernardino, CA
09 July 2019